INTRUSIVE GOD, DISRUPTIVE GOSPEL

Encountering the Divine *in the* Book of Acts

MATTHEW L. SKINNER

BrazosPress
a division of Baker Publishing Group
Grand Rapids, Michigan

© 2015 by Matthew L. Skinner

Published by Brazos Press
a division of Baker Publishing Group
P.O. Box 6287, Grand Rapids, MI 49516-6287
www.brazospress.com

Printed in the United States of America

Library of Congress Cataloging-in-Publication Data
Skinner, Matthew L., 1968–
    Intrusive God, disruptive gospel : encountering the divine in the Book of Acts / Matthew L. Skinner.
        pages cm
    Includes bibliographical references and index.
    ISBN 978-1-58743-375-7 (pbk.)
    1. Bible. Acts—Criticism, interpretation, etc. I. Title.
BS2625.52.S547 2015
226.6′07—dc23   2015010529

15   16   17   18   19   20   21   7   6   5   4   3   2   1

In keeping with biblical principles of creation stewardship, Baker Publishing Group advocates the responsible use of our natural resources. As a member of the Green Press Initiative, our company uses recycled paper when possible. The text paper of this book is composed in part of post-consumer waste.

Thank you, Beverly Roberts Gaventa,
my teacher and now friend

Contents

Preface

This book explores the Acts of the Apostles (customarily known by the simple title Acts), which appears immediately after the four Gospels in the New Testament. Acts continues the story the Gospels begin, the story of Jesus Christ. More accurately, Acts continues the story told in one of these Gospels in particular, the Gospel according to Luke. The same author wrote both books, making Acts a sequel. In Acts, the story of Jesus moves forward in the experiences of his followers—not all of them, but a few key figures who appear on the narrative's stage.

Acts shows very little interest in communicating details about these figures' lives. The book devotes much more attention to how their experiences—what they say, what they do, and what happens to them—say something about who God is and how God has acted and continues to act through the spread of the good news about Jesus Christ.

This book, the one you are reading now, explores Acts. But, like Acts, its interest also reaches further than retelling a story. As with Acts, this book is interested in directing your attention toward God and the good news ("the gospel") about what God accomplishes in Jesus Christ. That is, this book explores how Acts depicts God, or how Acts imagines God might be making a difference in the world because of what Jesus did and continues to do. Acts provides a lens through which we might see and consider God.

⌒⌒

This book is different from what I usually write. Since I am a biblical scholar, much of my interaction with the Acts of the Apostles involves a good amount of historical analysis, in an effort to uncover what was going on behind and around the story Acts tells and explain how Acts might have spoken to ancient readers in light of their knowledge and circumstances. This book, however, is relatively unconcerned with many aspects of the history behind Acts (why Acts was written, who the author was addressing, what problems Acts was trying to solve or create, and so on). I am more interested in exploring the story Acts tells to us today and how that story prompts us to consider who God is and how God operates.

Those topics interest me because I'm deeply curious about how the Bible shapes communities and how it informs and changes our understanding of who God is, what our faith is about, and what is possible in our lives. Acts tells a story about these things, but it is hardly an uncomplicated story. The story is fascinating, and it is determined to present readers with a gospel—and a God—that offers the possibility of new relationships and newfound hope, transforming lives and communities in the process. According to Acts, these transformations constitute part of the salvation God provides.

Acts looks back on transformations and discoveries rooted in the past, but in so doing it holds out hope for future ones too. Throughout this book I reflect on how our own encounters with God might be transformative in their own ways. These are my interpretations, which come from my efforts to learn from Acts and put my learning in conversation with my own life and the lives and perspectives of others.

I teach about Acts often to pastors, students, and congregations. Sometimes I meet people who resonate deeply with the book, finding it consistent with their experiences of a God who is near and active. More frequently, I encounter people who don't know what to do with Acts. Sermons in their churches seldom focus on the book. Some find Acts irredeemably shallow or even off-putting because of its focus on incredible stuff, such as fantastic miracles and daring, almost impossible heroism. Acts often describes easy solutions to problems and questions that, if our own lives are reliable indicators, do not lend themselves to neat and clean resolutions. Our lives and our thinking about God have a complexity that can leave us suspicious about simple answers. With this book I dig deeper into who God is in Acts so that you can better understand what Acts is saying about God and consider the portrait of God in Acts in light of how your own life has shaped your outlook on God. My primary hope is that I've written a book that helps you see more in Acts and that, as a result, Acts kindles for you deeper reflections and ongoing conversations with other people about who God is and how we know God.

This book is a result of innumerable conversations. Many people helped me write it, and they deserve my recognition.

Beverly Roberts Gaventa has taught me more about Acts than anyone else, which is why I dedicate the book to her. Her insights roam these pages.

Greg Carey first encouraged me to clarify specific ideas that I thought needed to be expressed in a book—this book. I had just completed a major writing project, and his determination to get me started quickly on my next one provided a creative spark and made me eager to dig in.

I made significant progress on the book and learned much about myself as an author while spending three weeks of summer 2010 as a writing fellow at the Center of Theological Inquiry in Princeton, New Jersey. I am grateful to the Center's director, William Storrar, for inviting me to participate in a writers' workshop led by Marilynne Robinson. The criticism and suggestions I received from her and my eleven writing companions proved to be invaluable; because of their insights, this book is much better than it would have been had I started the writing journey alone. Luther Seminary's academic dean at the time, Roland Martinson, enthusiastically supported my participation in this workshop. Jacqueline Lapsley, Gregory Bezilla, and their family showed me tremendous hospitality, making my time in Princeton more enjoyable and productive.

The Louisville Institute awarded me a generous Project Grant for Researchers in 2012–2013, creating the time I needed to bring my first draft almost to completion. My faculty colleagues and academic leadership at Luther Seminary were very supportive while I carved out time to write.

Barbara Joyner made it possible for me to take multiple short writing retreats, each one replete with generous hospitality. Never has working on a book been so fulfilling.

Eric Barreto, Greg Carey, Jaime Clark-Soles, Carey Newman, John Semmes, and Jenee Woodard read an early draft of the book; their careful attention and editorial suggestions made for a much-improved final product.

Notice the theme emerging here: the contributions of others. This book relies on many people's encouragement, support, and wisdom. Most of these contributors remain unnamed. I am grateful to my students and audiences in numerous classes, workshops, and congregations who have shared their questions and insights about the book of Acts with me. Countless people, all kinds of people, have shaped how I read Acts and have taught me what to look for in its pages. This is a good thing, since my book is committed to talking about God. We always need one another's insights if we're going to do that well.

Introduction

About that time no little disturbance broke out concerning the Way. (Acts 19:23)

"No little disturbance." The phrase introduces a story Acts tells about a riot in the ancient city of Ephesus. The deliberate understatement attracts our attention: it's a serious commotion. Indeed, in the scene that follows, the riot's instigators, joined by a throng of protestors, violently denounce what "the Way"—the expanding Christian movement that had recently come to Ephesus—will mean for the economic, religious, and political life of their city. The message of the Christian gospel and the actions of those who embrace it presage dramatic changes for many in Ephesus, and the rioters mean to nip this pesky movement in the bud in order to preserve their livelihood and their city's notable cultural reputation.

The hubbub in Ephesus—which we'll return to later in this book—resonates with a number of other episodes recounted in the book of Acts. Frequently those who announce the gospel of Jesus Christ do things that create or lead to large-scale disturbances. In one instance, a complaint ominously accuses them of "turning the world upside down" (Acts 17:6). What they teach about Jesus Christ asks people to embrace new religious, social, political, and economic values, sometimes putting both the proclaimers and their audiences at odds with the established social order. That social order—"the world" consisting of the various cultural pockets that together make up the

Roman Empire—doesn't appreciate being turned upside down. So it usually strikes back, not out of blind bigotry or petty disagreements over personal religious convictions but out of a keen awareness of just how influential this new religion will be if it is allowed to settle into a community and change how people live, worship, think about themselves, and spend their money. This gospel creates new realities among those who join it, even as it occasionally upsets their preexisting convictions about what's proper. Or what's possible.

The gospel is, in a word, disruptive.

People who live out this gospel say their God is bringing something new into being, something that challenges "the world"—the prevailing sense of "the way things are." As a result, the same word *disruptive* applies equally to God, as Acts tells the story. God intrudes. God breaks in. God interferes. Whether by sending people out to declare the good news about Jesus, preserving a shipload of desperate travelers during a violent storm, miraculously liberating persecuted missionaries from imprisonment, or creating communities where people gather together to worship, learn, and care for one another, the intrusive God who inhabits the pages of Acts repeatedly engenders "no little disturbance" in the lives of Jesus's followers and the wider population.

Does God still disrupt lives and societies today? Does the portrait of an intrusive God resemble the world we inhabit and the God we seek to know? If so, would that even be considered good news?

For a long time people have spoken about God as intimately engaged with and influencing the ordinary and extraordinary happenings of life. A belief in God's presence and activity plays a conspicuous role in many people's everyday piety. Consider these prayers: "God, give me the strength to get through this difficult day"; "Lord, see our soldiers safely through their tours of duty"; "Prosper for us the work of our hands."

Those types of beliefs also create problems for many of us. We rightly react warily to claims of divine activity as the cause of earthquakes and game-winning touchdown passes. More seriously, scientific developments in recent centuries have made certain claims about God's activity—God's role in influencing the events of our lives—more dubious or in need of more nuance than many of us churchgoers feel we can provide. Even when our religious convictions are not naive beliefs in a cosmic puppeteer who arranges every detail of human existence, many of us consider it difficult to speak realistically about God's activity. Add to this the cruel vulnerabilities of our lives reiterated daily in reports of wars, natural disasters, random violence, and climate change, and many of us become more and more uneasy about making statements to suggest God actually *does* much of anything in this calamitous world.

In this kind of environment, we might be excused for finding ourselves occasionally frustrated or even embarrassed by the book of Acts. For one thing, Acts tells a story in which Jesus's followers heal people by touching them or by having their shadows fall on them. Believers in Acts also see visions, find themselves physically swept up then miraculously deposited in distant cities, and even experience no ill effects from poisonous snakebites. The prodigious political and military might of the Roman Empire gets into the game but usually ends up powerless to thwart the preaching of God's word. We ask ourselves whether these things could really have happened, and if so, whether they occurred just as Acts describes. For some, it's acceptable to grant that Jesus could have had such experiences and been a miracle worker (after all, he was *Jesus*); but when Acts says that his followers did the same things, it might imply this kind of stuff lies within the reach of any and all Christians—past, present, and future.

If it's not within our reach, are we still in touch with the same God today? Has God changed since then? Have the standard operating procedures been revised? Are we expecting the wrong things? Some Christians claim Acts describes what we should all expect. But what about those of us who find the action in Acts more alien or incredible? If the book of Acts appears foreign to our lives and experiences, it becomes difficult to figure out what we are supposed to make of what Acts says about the way things are with God and the world.

That's where the book you have in your hands comes in. Its purpose is to explore the theological vision we encounter in Acts. By "theological vision," I mean the perspectives Acts takes on God's ways of disturbing business as usual. These perspectives can shape our understanding of who God is; they might enliven the expectations we have about God and how God might connect to our lives. By exploring these expectations, we can become more creative, more imaginative, more perceptive, and even sometimes more suspicious in our outlook on where and how we might look for or encounter God. Seeking signs of God, we might follow where Acts points, or we might head in different directions. In either case, Acts will make us consider the question of what we think we're looking for.

Maybe, then, our question shouldn't be, "Has God changed since Acts was written?" but instead, "Have our imaginations and expectations about God become too confined? Too one-dimensional? Too cautious?" Acts might prompt us to ask deeper questions about what is real, and about what God might make possible in our lives and our neighbors' lives.

While in this book I'll pursue how Acts can contribute to our own theological perspectives, I'm very aware of the ways in which Acts provokes all sorts of questions, especially historical questions such as "Did it really happen just like that?" and "Why did the author write such a book?" Questions like these are very important, yet this book will not devote attention to offering answers that respect their complexity. I should say, however, that we miss the point of Acts if we assume that we must classify it as either a precise historical chronicle or an amusing sampling of ancient superstitions. At the same time, we benefit from knowing something about where Acts sits in history. It was written within a decade or two of the year 100, during a period between two major revolts that cost the lives of huge numbers of Jews and magnified negative perceptions of Jews and Judaism across the Roman Empire. Communities of Jesus's followers, at that time still in contentious and often regrettable processes of separating themselves from Judaism, were coming to terms with what it meant to live in protracted waiting for Jesus's return and for the final fulfillment of all God's promises. By then, probably everyone who knew Jesus during his public ministry around the year 30 had died, and so had much of the next generation. How should the current and coming generations of this movement, this religion, regard themselves and understand what their churches are to do? How will the movement survive, and what should it look like? What should these people expect from God?

The historical issues are important because Acts was originally written to address ancient audiences asking those tough questions about their purpose and identity in light of the particular place they occupied in an unfolding history. (We still ask similar questions for ourselves now. Or we should.) In speaking to these audiences, Acts does not promise to tell the complete, definitive history of the early church. It tries to describe God as the church's creator and preserver. Like most books worth reading, it does this with no small amount of flourish and occasional embellishment. Acts clearly includes some historical reporting, for it speaks of real people and places we can learn more about. Our exploration of the book will pay attention, therefore, to those details. Knowing some information about the culture in ancient Athens, Corinth, and Ephesus, for example, will help us make better sense of the action that transpires in those settings.

Over and over again, Acts will put forth a basic understanding of God as intimately involved in the spread of the gospel message and present among the communities of faith that the gospel creates. Acts asserts God's activity in the growth, movement, changes, and struggles experienced by the early church. It was not a strange thing in the ancient world to believe that invisible forces or divine beings guide or influence history; what makes Acts distinctive in this setting is its insistence that the God made known in the history of ancient Israel and in Jesus Christ is the One who does so. Acts looks back at the earliest years of Christianity—during periods before anyone even called it "Christianity" to label it as a clearly defined development—and sees in them a demonstration of God's active, persistent commitment to bring salvation to the world and to make that salvation known.

How, then, does the story of Acts put forth its "theological vision"? We should keep two things in mind. First, the whole story conveys the theological vision. Not only what people say about God but also the rest of the story—the narrated drama, the repetitions, the unspooling of promises, even the silences—make claims both overt and subtle about God being discernible in the experiences of Jesus's followers. Acts sees God made manifest in these experiences whether they entail success or failure. Acts sees God manifest in the preaching of "the good news" about Jesus, "the gospel," and in how people respond to it. "The gospel" and "God" are not identical, of course, but the gospel discloses who God is by expressing what God's intentions look like; we see these intentions when people experience healing, inclusion, forgiveness, and hope. Acts depicts the gospel as not only a message but also something embodied in Jesus's followers, as individuals and mostly as the communities they form.

Second, Acts recognizes the mystery that comes with talking about God. The book does not delineate exactly where and how God affects people and events, nor can we read it as a field guide offering an exhaustive, timeless, or unambiguous depiction of God and God's intentions. Acts is a narrative, a story. As a story, it invites readers to live with and watch this God for a while. Acts tells its story in a confident voice out of a commitment to demonstrate God's reliability. As we will see in pages to come, however, the people we meet in Acts often find themselves having a challenging time keeping pace with God; they sometimes cannot get their heads around how God is leading or speaking in an event until after it has concluded. The impression left is one of Christians looking backward and trying to discern God's business even as they look forward and imagine what might happen next. This can, admittedly, be a risky or even self-fulfilling way of making a case about God. We will consider some of the challenges Acts poses for how we think about God, but for now it is enough to note that the people in Acts often lack certainty about where things are headed or what specific purpose might be in view. God's ways are not easily anticipated. As Acts exhorts us to look for God, it also reminds us of the incomplete and elusive character of our talk about God.

Through its relentless attention to what God makes possible through Jesus Christ and the spread of the Christian gospel, Acts invites us to think about God in the choices we make and the promises we cling to as we live out our own faith. As we set priorities for our futures, counsel children, organize communities and congregations, or merely figure out what we have to look forward to, we should converse with Acts smartly yet creatively, always with a sense of wonder and with an acknowledgment of the limits of what we can know.

As we attend to what Acts shows and tells us about God and God's intentions, we can find fresh ways of imagining God's presence in our own experiences.

Any disturbances that may come from our exploration might not be as raucous as a riot in Ephesus. You might not feel an emotional rush on par with all the narrow escapes described in Acts, as if you've survived a dramatic shipwreck. Nevertheless, reading Acts and allowing it to fuel reflections on God can still be revolutionary and visceral activities if the book leads us into deeper awareness of what it means to live faithfully and responsively to God. When that happens, all sorts of things become possible.

Road Map

As You Read This Book

If I may offer some advice to get you situated before we turn to Acts, I think you will find the book I've written most helpful if you do the following:

1. Remember that it deals only with portions of the Acts of the Apostles. I have chosen twenty-six passages from Acts. If you add these passages together, the number of words they contain constitutes only a little more than half of a much longer narrative. (I occasionally comment on how a passage connects to other parts of Acts. Use the index at the end of the book if you want to see where I mention these other parts.) The passages we will explore in detail represent some of the variety of material in Acts, and they help us keep our focus on the question of how Acts prompts us to imagine God. But Acts is a larger story. To keep this in sight, I strongly recommend that you read all of the book of Acts before or as you read this book. The five additional "road map" chapters I've provided will keep you oriented to where individual passages fit within the wider narrative and thematic structure of Acts to help you relate segments of the story to the whole.

2. Keep a Bible available as you read. While my chapters interact closely with specific passages from Acts, I usually do not summarize all the action. My chapters assume that you have already slightly familiarized yourself with the passage(s) or are consulting Acts as you work through this book. When I quote from Acts in the chapter headings or anywhere else, I use the New Revised Standard Version of the Bible (NRSV). Even if you have a different translation of the Bible, you should still have no trouble keeping track of what I say here and how it connects to the passages we're investigating.

3. Do not expect an answer to every question about "what really happened." Some people find reason to believe Acts narrates events as they really occurred, more or less, nearly two thousand years ago. Others are convinced that Acts contains mainly legendary stories meant to illustrate convictions about God and the church more than to relate a precise, factual account. It is a mistake to assume that Acts must entirely be either one of these or the other. It is also a mistake, when it comes to how ancient writers understood history and history telling, to assign "fact" and "fiction" labels as totally separate or distinguishable categories. Other books about Acts can help with sorting through those questions; some of them appear in the "For Further Reading" section at the end. I have tried to write this book in a way that will make it useful to a broad variety of readers—those who see no legendary elements in Acts, those who do, and those who do not worry about such matters. My focus is to approach Acts from a different angle, to ask about the God we might encounter in the story.

Acts 1:1–11

Waiting to Go

He ordered them not to leave Jerusalem, but to wait there
for the promise of the Father. (Acts 1:4)

The Acts of the Apostles begins where the Gospel according to Luke
left off: with an emerging recognition that God is creating new possibilities, that God is bringing long-promised things to fruition. Truly,
it's a whole new world.

Backing up a step, before getting to these new realities, there is the
matter of the connection between the end of Luke and the beginning
of Acts. As the first two verses of Acts indicate, the book presents itself
as a sequel to Luke, written by the same author to the same reader,
an otherwise unknown "Theophilus" (compare Luke 1:1–4). The
stories told in the two books connect right as the risen Jesus Christ
leaves his followers and commissions them to work on his behalf.
Luke ends with an ascension; Acts begins with one.

At the juncture between the books, as Jesus ascends, the fullness of what God has done through Jesus's life and death remains
undefined and unrealized. The same is true concerning what God
will do through the lives of Jesus's followers. But expectations are
high. The final chapters of Luke got our attention: someone recently
executed as an enemy of the state was raised from the dead and appeared to his friends. Death, life's great certainty, was upended. In its

stories about the resurrected Jesus, the final chapter of Luke's Gospel offered morsels of insight into what Jesus's cross and resurrection might mean, and it divulged just a few hints about what will come next in post-Easter times.

As Acts begins, we find ourselves waiting to hear more about what exactly God has accomplished through Jesus and what might come next. Several of Jesus's promises ring in our ears. For example, just prior to his arrest, he said to the twelve apostles,

> You are those who have stood by me in my trials; and I confer on you, just as my Father has conferred on me, a kingdom, so that you may eat and drink at my table in my kingdom, and you will sit on thrones judging the twelve tribes of Israel. [Then, turning to Simon Peter, Jesus continued,] Simon, Simon, listen! Satan has demanded to sift all of you like wheat, but I have prayed for you that your own faith may not fail; and you, when once you have turned back, strengthen your brothers. (Luke 22:28–32)

After his resurrection, Jesus told the wider company of his disciples (his remaining apostles as well as other followers),

> Thus it is written, that the Messiah is to suffer and to rise from the dead on the third day, and that repentance and forgiveness of sins is to be proclaimed in his name to all nations, beginning from Jerusalem. You are witnesses of these things. And see, I am sending upon you what my Father promised; so stay here in the city until you have been clothed with power from on high. (Luke 24:46–49)

Death overpowered. Promises of a kingdom. Promises of power. Promises of forgiveness extended to all. Promises of work to be done. We expect God to do something, therefore, to equip Jesus's friends and to call them into action. We expect Peter (maybe a surprising choice, given his inconsistent track record as a disciple in the Gospel according to Luke) to provide leadership to strengthen Jesus's followers. We expect big things from the apostles at the beginning of Acts, because Jesus said so.

In another sense, however, Acts does not pick up exactly where Luke left off. Jesus ascended to heaven at the end of Luke's Gospel after making a few brief appearances to his followers during the course of a single day. When we read about the ascension in Acts, the clock has been turned back. Acts first describes Jesus still physically present with his followers, interacting with them in Jerusalem over a protracted, forty-day period. (Neither the Gospel of Luke nor Acts ever explains the discrepancy in how much time elapses between Jesus's resurrection and ascension.) During the forty-day period, Jesus makes a few additional promises before disappearing into the sky. These promises inform his followers about what will soon involve them. He tells them to wait in Jerusalem until they are "baptized with the Holy Spirit," reaffirming that they "will receive power when the Holy Spirit has come."

The power he promises will come from God, as did Jesus's power to effect change during the course of his ministry (see Acts 10:38). This power will have a purpose: to make these ordinary people into Jesus's witnesses across the Roman world. As witnesses, they will tell what they know and what they have seen; they will also make Jesus and his intentions manifest in how they conduct themselves. Their witnessing will begin in Jerusalem and move throughout the broader region, the Roman province of Judea. It will go northward into Samaria (a territory not exactly on good terms with the kind of people who constitute Jesus's current followers, Judean and Galilean Jews) and ultimately to points unknown, "the ends of the earth."

They must be eager. They must be terrified.

New things stand at the threshold, then, at the beginning of Acts. According to Jesus's promises to his followers, his departure does not conclude but initiates the next chapter in a grand narrative about the salvation God makes possible. While Jesus's words include an instruction to remain in Jerusalem for the time being, his dominant thrust is descriptive: he simply informs his friends of what God will do and what they will do as a result. His statements and promises outnumber the one request. Power, Holy Spirit, testimony about Jesus and forgiveness of sins, participation in God's kingdom, expansion across cultural and geopolitical lines, opposition (implied by the courtroom flavor of the word *witnesses* and stated clearly by

Jesus back in Luke 12:11–12 and 21:12–17)—again, big things lie
ahead for these people.

The promises' magnitude creates a contrast to his followers' inability to grasp how it all might unfold, as illustrated by their entirely reasonable but not-quite-appropriate question about what is
going to happen and when: "Lord, is this the time when you will
restore the kingdom to Israel?" Jesus promised a kingdom back in
Luke 22:28–32, but he never guaranteed he could give answers about
when that might happen. He equips his followers with promises,
not schedules.

They will have some catching up to do as the story progresses if
they are to keep pace with what God has in store. For now, however,
clearly Jesus's ascension will not mean the immediate arrival of the
fullness of God's kingdom, the realization of all God's intentions
for humanity's well-being. But neither will the ascension mean the
cessation of Jesus's ministry or the suspension of God's activity to
set the world free from all kinds of oppression. Two men in white
robes, heavenly messengers, reassure Jesus's followers that he will
return in a manner as unmistakable as that of his departure. Still
another big thing to come. And again, no one knows when. Yet the
time for looking into the sky in wonder has ended.

The beginning of any book can set the tone for what follows. Acts
starts with strong theological statements about God's intentions. The
boldness of some, such as "You will receive power," makes us take
notice, especially when the most recent display of divine power was a
resurrection. The open-endedness of other things Jesus says, such as
what exactly it will entail for Jesus's followers to be his "witnesses,"
invites readers to settle in, to watch and learn along with the people
who inhabit the pages of Acts. In the boldness and mystery about
them, the statements hold God responsible to make God's intentions
known and effective. Acts begins by fixing everyone's attention and
expectations upon God, even as it makes clear that people will play
a part in God's objectives.

What about the execution of these plans, the next step? The next
step into what promises to be a great and glorious future brought

about by the culmination of "the kingdom of God"—will this happen right away? No. First, everyone waits.

Fulfillment will come, but after a waiting period. When the two messengers in robes call Jesus's followers back to their senses after he disappears, they do not tell them to get to work. Although there is urgency in the messengers' admonishment to stop staring slack-jawed into the sky and pondering everything, the moment's urgency is not a call to action. It is a call to wait. The first great act in the Acts of the Apostles is to walk back to Jerusalem and let time pass. Eventually, the apostles and the rest of Jesus's followers will be moving outward and bearing witness to Jesus in the world-altering power of the Holy Spirit, but not now. Even as Jesus's and the angels' words generate momentum for action to come, his people stay put as instructed.

We may find the waiting at the beginning of Acts easy to skip over, as a brief narrative hesitation to build suspense for the eventual coming of the Holy Spirit during the Jewish festival of Pentecost at the beginning of Acts 2. Yet the interval conveys an important lesson about how God will interact with these people. Presumably the Holy Spirit could have come immediately after Jesus's ascension, but God waits a little more than one week's time.

Why the delay? For one thing, waiting often proves wise when people try to make sense of where and how God is accompanying them. Waiting reminds us of our dependence on God and the limitations of our ability to see and know God. By waiting, Jesus's followers begin to learn that they need to be a responsive community, a community that waits upon God to initiate. Whether they return to Jerusalem from the ascension with eager energy or paralyzing fear, we do not know. It's probably both. All we know is that their job, for now, is to hang on.

This waiting has an active quality to it, going beyond merely sitting around and contemplating the past and the future. Further into the chapter, we will learn that they wait secluded in a "room upstairs" where they are "constantly devoting themselves to prayer" along with others who followed Jesus, both men and women (1:12–14). Also, Peter begins his work of strengthening the community (recall Luke

22:32) by leading the process whereby the whole group (consisting of about 120 people) selects two candidates for filling the spot among the twelve apostles vacated by Judas Iscariot (Acts 1:15–26). The group remains sequestered yet expectant. In their waiting they obey Jesus's commands, but they also express a readiness for what will come.

They wait in a context of enormous and not fully explained expectations. They must feel like anything is possible now as they breathlessly anticipate the new realities that the risen and ascended Jesus has declared. To live like this—waiting—requires just as much courage as if Jesus had told them to go out immediately and change the world on their own. The waiting period trains them to be available and attentive so they might respond as followers when the time comes.

Much of Acts depicts Christians as responsive people, people who watch for God's lead. They are not puppets but agents, prompted by God to tell what they have seen, to report and give evidence of the new realities God has brought about through Jesus. The courage these people exhibit in doing so throughout all sorts of situations in Acts leads some readers to understand the book as a depiction of human heroism to spread the gospel. But this view misses the point. As the opening verses of Acts prepare us for the story to come, as dust has hardly begun to settle on the rumpled burial cloths left behind in Jesus's empty tomb, promises of what *God* will do in and through Jesus's followers fill the air.

For many people I know, waiting to make a decision or to put a plan into action proves a frustrating thing to do, because it feels like indecision, weakness, or wasted time. Once you start waiting, how do you know when it's time to stop? The beginning of Acts seems to suggest that you'll know, as long as you remain attentive and anticipant as you wait. Waiting isn't always the best course of action, but in the beginning of Acts, there's nothing else these people can do. For them, it's part of learning to be a disciple.

Jesus's followers wait not because they see it as their only option, not because they need to figure out everything before they take a first step, but because they expect God to open up opportunities and new realities. When God does, they, along with many others, will be privileged to play vital parts.

Acts 2:1–21

Making Sense of Things

> All were amazed and perplexed, saying to one another,
> "What does this mean?" (Acts 2:12)

If a roomful of people given the ability to speak foreign languages sounds impressive, try to imagine the splash a community full of prophets might make.

The terms *prophet* and *prophecy* worry many of us, filling our minds with memories of wild-eyed doomsayers wearing sandwich boards in Times Square or late-night commercials touting the wonders of psychic hotlines. The words usually mean something altogether different in Acts, however, for prophecy can refer to interpreting the present as often as it refers to foretelling what's to come. Prophets perceive in particular the relevance of the present for an unfolding, anticipated future. They also act, playing roles in the realization of the future. Prophecy emerges as an important theme in Acts as a result of what happens during the Jewish harvest festival called Pentecost: Jesus's followers, along with the thousands who join them, become a community of prophets when they receive the Holy Spirit, the Spirit of God. This Spirit empowers them to explain the significance of events that occur in their midst; they claim that those events offer evidence of God bringing new realities to fruition through the life, death, resurrection, and glorification of Jesus Christ. They live out the gospel in their bold speech, mutual care, worship, and service.

As the scene gets underway in Acts 2, a crowd gathers and marvels at a large group of Galileans speaking in foreign languages about "God's deeds of power." The amazement expressed by the crowd comes hand-in-hand with a slight toward the people proclaiming the good news: these people are from Galilee, of all places, people whom popular caricatures belittle as ignorant bumpkins.

The experience nevertheless transfixes the crowd and leaves them asking, "What does this mean?" The masses are not taken by the sound like a violent, dangerous wind and the sight of something like tongues of flames appearing among Jesus's followers, as those phenomena come and go in a private setting without anyone paying them much attention. The crowd in the public venue wants, rather, an explanation for the stunning symphony of proclamations about God's deeds of power. All these languages! Spoken by Galileans! The observers' question goes beyond wondering how this could be happening; they ask, "What does this mean?" What is the significance of this? What's really going on?

Everything that follows in the scene attempts to answer this basic question. Peter explains that the unusual display of multilingual pronouncements points to the presence of God's Spirit within him and his companions. What does this mean, then? It means God is here. The time of God's salvation—a salvation we will explore more carefully in the next few chapters—has arrived. As he provides more information, Peter goes beyond identifying the Spirit's presence; his words also demonstrate what the Spirit empowers him to do. As we shall see, not only does he tell; he also shows. After all, he's a prophet.

Peter chooses a passage from the prophet Joel in the Jewish scriptures to help explain what is happening. He does not quote the words of the prophet verbatim. Rather, a subtle reshaping of Joel 2:28–32a makes it more fitting to the current occasion, allowing Joel's old words to speak more appropriately to this new occurrence. By comparing Joel 2:28–32a to Acts 2:17–21, we see Peter revises the scriptural passage in at least three noteworthy ways, all of which contribute to answering the crowd's initial question.

First, he changes the opening clause of Joel's statement from "After these things" to "In the last days." Many centuries earlier, Joel wrote about a series of events that would eventuate in the ultimate arrival of the day of the Lord. Peter emphasizes the outpouring of God's Spirit not as the conclusion of a series of events but as an indicator of the beginning of a concluding, culminating era in human history. The arrival of God's Spirit means the times have changed; God is bringing something to its fullness.

Second, Peter inserts the word *my* before "slaves." While Joel referred to "slaves" explicitly as a socioeconomic class, Peter broadens the sense of who belongs in this category. The people who receive God's Spirit live as God's possession, all of them enlisted to participate in God's works. The Spirit, then, has a purpose in coming to these people who follow Jesus Christ, designating them as people in God's service during this new era in which God brings salvation to pass.

Third, Peter adds "and they shall prophesy" at the end of Acts 2:18. The repetition turns this simple statement into an emphatic refrain. Peter reiterates why God's Spirit is bestowed on "all flesh," given to young and old, to women and men: so they will prophesy.

Peter thus makes a few alterations to Joel's declarations about God's Spirit so they will fit, or be more precisely meaningful for, the current occasion. He does not correct or misquote Joel as much as he adapts Joel's old words to speak to new circumstances. Simply repeating the old words would not quite explain much of anything by itself. Peter's primary impulse is to make sense of a new context (the events of Pentecost and the emerging era of God's salvation through Jesus Christ). He does so by describing the current conditions as an arena in which God operates and can be recognized. In the coming of the Spirit, God makes a new reality possible in ways both familiar and disruptive.

In the passage from Joel, Peter thus finds a resource for answering his audience's question. Corresponding with the three revisions he makes to Joel's words, Peter's explanation does at least three things.

First, he interprets the time. "What does this mean?" the crowd asks. Peter replies: the unleashing of God's Spirit indicates the beginning of a new day in human history. Here, in the days immediately following Jesus's death, resurrection, and exaltation, a new and ultimate chapter begins in the story of God's interactions with humanity.

Peter also interprets the community created by the Spirit. "What does this mean?" In reply, Peter tells the crowd the Spirit marks Jesus's followers—each one—as belonging to God. They are God's slaves, speaking and working on God's behalf. Referring to enslavement in a positive light might shock the audience, as most in the Roman-occupied world would understand the dishonor that usually came with being a slave. When Peter embraces this identity, he further illuminates the disruptive nature of the Spirit's arrival.

Third, Peter interprets the work of the Spirit-filled community. "What does this mean?" Peter boldly answers that the foreign languages are not an instance of trickery or mass hysteria. God is present, equipping people to communicate truth about God's deeds. The Spirit prompts them to engage in *prophecy*. The community of faith is a community of prophets here to speak, act, and interpret.

We learn about prophesying by watching Peter do it. His interpretation of the day's events in light of Joel's words offers an example of prophecy. More follows later in the chapter when he will explain to the crowd that the Holy Spirit comes from Jesus, the same One who was crucified, resurrected, and exalted. The coming of the Spirit announces Jesus's ongoing presence within his followers, in their speech and activity. Peter's brand of prophecy is truth telling. It is interpretation: naming the ways and places where God's salvation is realized, where God's presence and influence can be encountered. It is insisting that humanity's existence and the life of God do not exist in separate planes; rather, they are intertwined, each a part of the other.

Why is prophecy necessary? Because making sense of present events is necessary, whether those events strike us as extraordinary or mundane. Peter makes sense of the peculiar experience of multilingual preachers from Galilee by making theological sense of it—by finding in it evidence of God's salvation as well as evidence for Peter's and others' roles in announcing it. Because the Spirit has come, Joel and Peter conclude together, "Everyone who calls on the name of the Lord shall be saved." In the present, Peter sees a trail into a future God prepares. Peter's message draws from promises and images rooted in the *past*. He draws from prior testimony about God's activity (Scripture from Joel, as well as Peter's own testimony or memory about Jesus). He attends to the *present* realities that first provoke the crowd's question (emboldened Galilean preachers). He also uses ideas and promises that connect to the *future*, for all of Peter's Pentecost sermon extending through 2:40 points toward the salvation God will ultimately accomplish. The thread meaningfully woven through past, present, and future shows Peter's audience how current experiences belong among memories of God's past assurances and future intentions.

Peter is at pains, then, to show that the events of the day point beyond themselves to attest Jesus as Lord and Messiah and to announce the present availability of God's salvation. While Acts might make this task appear easy, the challenge of affirming Jesus as Lord and Messiah is anything but that. What sounds established to us who benefit from two thousand years of Christian history would strike Peter's audience as quite unexpected. But prophets have eyes to see God's penchant for acting in astounding and disruptive ways.

People sometimes assume that theology involves gazing into ancient wisdom, that it originates in reciting traditions of the past. They associate theology primarily with books, inherited knowledge, or deep meditations on the nature of existence. While these things have their value, we must note that in this scene Peter is primarily neither an interpreter of Scripture nor a sage dispensing arcane pronouncements. First and foremost he interprets the present time by speaking about God's connection to it. Scripture gives him language for doing so. His speech reminds us that as long as it is Christians' business to speak about where life's occurrences might or might not fit within the grand scheme of God's relationship to the world, the need for theology (describing God and God's ways of encountering the world) and prophecy (declaring God's relevance for our and our neighbors' lives) never ends. Theology and prophecy take account of new material that presents itself to us through the course of human experience. Every day people look at events around them and ask, "What does this mean?" or "What am I supposed to do with this?" The book of Acts offers an array of stories about Jesus's followers trying to answer these questions for people in different circumstances.

Prophets speak truth into the confusion generated on Pentecost. They do the same when economies falter or relationships fall apart; prophets speak also to good situations, such as thriving communities or people given opportunities for a fresh start. Prophets—all those who follow Jesus and share in the Holy Spirit—direct our attention in our current circumstances to see where we might rediscover the availability of God's salvation or God's commitment to renew and restore. They have eyes to see God's presence and to reassert God's priorities when others might be too disoriented or distracted to do so.

Peter does not do his prophetic work alone or as an extraordinary figure. Through his reference to Joel he refers to a community full of Spirit-empowered visionaries and dreamers. Others too are equipped to make and convey meaning about the world and God's commitment to it. Peter insists that God's Spirit flows in all directions, filling people across social boundaries. The many languages of Pentecost invite people from various places representing multitudes of cultures. The Spirit doesn't undo differences among people; the Spirit blesses those differences. God's Spirit empowers interpretation that happens corporately, not merely handed down from a single charismatic authority figure.

The events of Pentecost do not appear as an entirely unique occurrence in Acts. Other scenes, several of which we will explore in coming chapters, also describe the Holy Spirit mobilizing Jesus's followers and inaugurating new and unforeseen directions for ministry and community. The Spirit continues to point believers toward new horizons. These horizons are sometimes geographical (new places, new audiences) and sometimes ministerial (new dimensions to the work of Jesus's followers). Rarely do the characters of Acts set out toward these horizons without receiving a prompt or a shove. Rarely can they answer a question like "What does this mean?" until they find opportunity to gather information and ruminate upon it with other believers. When Acts describes Christian communities moving into new stages of their existence and taking on new members, those events do not interpret themselves. Only infrequently does God, Jesus, or the Spirit directly speak in Acts. Usually God relies on the people in the story to make statements about God's intentions or activity.

Peter's sermon describes who God is and how God operates. He invites his hearers (and us, the readers) to apprehend God's salvation playing itself out in the stunning events of the day but also in anything else occurring during these ongoing "last days." After all, the same Spirit who initiates the miraculous speaking in foreign tongues at Pentecost also creates—when the scene concludes in 2:42–47—a community marked by its fellowship, worship, unity, and charity. The daily life of that community may look more ordinary than the sights and sounds that set the Pentecost story into motion, but Peter's prophetic sermon trains our eyes to interpret such a community as yet another sign of God's transformative presence.

When the topic is God or interpreting God's presence, we should be wary of any who speak nonchalantly or cavalierly. Accordingly Acts, even with all the book's confidence, recognizes the difficulties. When we widen our vision and read about the events of Pentecost as part of a larger story, we discover that even the gift of the Spirit does not remove all the existential and theological struggles from life. Peter might appear incredibly impressive and certain in this scene, but he and the other luminaries we meet in Acts do not receive all the answers when the Spirit comes. Throughout the story they must live into God's future, themselves susceptible to error and reliant on others to make sense of God's ways. This is the messy yet necessary work of all God's people. Acts never promises that the charge to prophesy gives Christians full knowledge, nor that our attempts to describe God's ways are foolproof.

The giving of the Holy Spirit, with accompanying sights and sounds to signal divine presence, may exemplify God's dramatic disturbance of the status quo, but when the human beings in Acts get down to business, their prophetic work often involves less spectacle. It is no less remarkable and no less influential as a result. The eyes and insights bestowed at Pentecost carry a promise: God will be known in the world not only through dramatic events and gifted preachers but also—even primarily—through the ordinary words and lives of all God's people. Remember, they're a prophetic bunch.

Acts 2:22–41

Keeping an Old Promise

For the promise is for you, for your children, and for all
who are far away. (Acts 2:39)

The loud noises and freakish sights accompanying the coming of the
Holy Spirit (Acts 2:2–3) are hardly the only disruptive elements of
the Pentecost story. More fireworks will come.

The previous chapter discussed the beginning of Peter's sermon
on Pentecost and jumped ahead in Acts 2 to note the community
of faith created in the sermon's immediate aftermath. This chapter
deals with what happens in between, the rest of Peter's sermon. The
sermon often escapes many readers' attention; some just skip over it.

They skip it because it is not the most engaging sermon ever to be
preached. It repeatedly looks back to the Psalms to establish its point
about Jesus being superior to King David. To some, it looks more
like an argument drawing on scriptural texts to prove obscure points
than a sermon describing God or inspiring an audience.

But that point of view overlooks Peter's persistent focus on God.
Notice his claims: God performed "deeds of power, wonders, and
signs" through Jesus (2:22). God "freed [Jesus] from death" (2:24; see
also 2:32). God promised that a descendant of David would one day
hold authority (2:30). Despite the crucifixion of Jesus, God "made
him both Lord and Messiah" (2:36). Peter encapsulates Jesus's life,

death, resurrection, and ascension so as to paint the whole story with a *theological* brush—Peter insists Jesus's life story ultimately is about God's involvement and God's commitment.

In doing so, Peter asks his audience in Jerusalem to adopt a new perspective on Jesus. His sermon calls for recognition from them. Wading into topics that will appear in future sermons (including the one in Acts 3, to be explored in a coming chapter), Peter wants them to recognize that God's purposes cannot be deterred by Jesus's crucifixion and the human ignorance that brought about this cruel execution. Although crucifixion branded Jesus as an enemy of the empire and as one outside the bounds of acceptability, Peter tells his audience to recognize that what Jesus spoke about and embodied in his ministry came from God and continues now through Jesus's reign as Lord, the One exalted by God. With the coming of the Holy Spirit on Pentecost, they must recognize that promises about the fullness of this reign continue now, described in the witness offered by Jesus's followers. God remains present and involved. (Acts keeps God, Jesus, and the Spirit distinct. Remember, Christians did not come up with the Trinity as a way of explaining the connections between Jesus, the Holy Spirit, and the One Jesus calls "Father" until long after the New Testament was written. Acts describes Father, Son, and Spirit working in tight, overlapping communion. The book thus provides the raw material, we might say, for eventually understanding Jesus as God, even though it never states it so bluntly.)

The sermon's repeated appeals for recognition explain why, after the hearers ask what they should do in 2:37, Peter's response begins, "Repent." Repentance means more than changed behavior or expressions of remorse. At root, the word refers to a changed mind. It means embracing a new way of understanding something. Sure, a new understanding may lead to a new morality down the road, but first and foremost Peter tells the assembled Jewish audience to recognize God at work in Jesus Christ and therefore to recognize Jesus's authority to announce and enact God's salvation. "Rethink what happened," Peter essentially says, not long after Jesus's resurrection and ascension, "and then imagine new possibilities in what God continues to do."

When Peter exhorts people to be saved "from this corrupt generation," he makes almost the same point. In Luke's Gospel, when

Jesus spoke of "this generation," he emphasized a prevalent condition among humanity: an inability to perceive God's activity (see, for example, Luke 11:29–32, 50–51). In decrying corruption, Peter focuses not on immoral behavior as much as on a more basic disposition of faithlessness and opposition to God. According to Deuteronomy 32:4–5, the sharpest contrast to a corrupt, or "crooked," humanity is a faithful God. Peter tells his listeners to see it his way: the life, death, resurrection, and ascension of Jesus express God's faithfulness to humanity. He calls people to move from their ignorance about what God has done to an embrace of God's faithfulness manifested in Jesus Christ and further asserted in the Holy Spirit's arrival. That's repentance.

Acts devotes much attention to God's faithfulness; at its core, the story of Jesus demonstrates God's reliability, God's commitment to keep promises. This attention comes in multiple ways.

Everything about the Pentecost scene in Acts 2 exists as a fulfilled promise. Jesus told his followers to expect the Holy Spirit as "the promise of the Father" in 1:4. He also referred to the coming of "power from on high" as "what [his] Father promised" in Luke 24:49.

Later in Acts, as Paul preaches a sermon in Antioch of Pisidia to an audience in a synagogue, we see similarities with Peter's Pentecost sermon, which refers to the book of Psalms to indicate God fulfilling established expectations. Paul in the later sermon will refer to Jesus as the Savior from David's lineage whom God promised to provide for the people of Israel (13:23). The good news about Jesus, accomplished and validated in his resurrection, fulfills "what God promised" to the people of Israel many generations prior to Jesus's lifetime (13:32–33).

More generally, the Gospel of Luke roots the coming of Jesus in the larger story of God's reliability. When people in Luke 1–2 recognized the significance of John the Baptizer and Jesus, when the two were conceived and born, they extolled God as a promise keeper. Mary (Luke 1:46–55) and Zechariah (Luke 1:67–79) described God as remembering mercy and covenantal pledges. Simeon and Anna had similar responses (Luke 2:25–38). Jesus launched his ministry in

Nazareth with a statement about scriptural promises finding their fulfillment in his work (Luke 4:16–21).

Why should people be concerned with the question of whether God keeps promises? The point is not to box God into a strict set of definitions and expectations to make God utterly predictable. Nor is it about trying to prove Christianity is true. Rather, confidence in God's dependability makes a key statement about who God is; it reaffirms God as a legitimate focus of our faith. Why should anyone put hope in a God who lacks the power or resolve to deliver on promises? Why trust a God who might terminate agreements or change the terms when the going gets rough? God's reliability makes the good news about God's disruptive activity good.

Neither is Acts merely interested in cataloging God's past accomplishments to construct an impressive résumé showing God's longstanding greatness. Acts insists that the content or benefits of God's promises are available now; they can be apprehended. Notice Peter's statement near the end of this passage: "The promise is for you, for your children, and for all who are far away, everyone whom the Lord our God calls." Christians do not regard the good news about Jesus as merely God making good on an old pledge to David or to Moses. Peter speaks about promises with a very wide scope. They belong to his Jewish audience. They belong to the audience's offspring, including those not yet born. They belong to "all who are far away." They apply now. They apply broadly.

Acts describes a God whose reach and concern stretch worldwide. Whose promises benefit all. Whose old promises provide foundations for hope about the future. Whose grace welcomes newcomers, allowing them to share in a much older history. Christians stand in a long trajectory of people who have sought out and encountered God.

But exactly which "promise" does Peter have in mind in 2:39—this promise still available to all? Although Peter does not provide a clear statement, the rest of his sermon fleshes it out. Part of the promise is *salvation*, the reassurance that God's people will be preserved and will thrive. Just as the citation from Joel in Acts 2:17–21 culminated with the statement that the outpouring of God's Spirit corresponds to salvation for "everyone who calls on the name of the

Lord," likewise Peter's final words on Pentecost are "Save yourselves from this corrupt generation." The promise that salvation has come frames the sermon. The coming of the Spirit, Peter insists, offers a reliable demonstration of this.

Acts speaks about salvation to reassert God's commitment to people and to maintain that this commitment sometimes reorders a society's prevailing values. Following the way characters in Luke 1–2 speak of God's salvation and Jesus as Savior (Luke 1:46–55, 67–79; 2:28–32), Acts uses salvation language to indicate God's actions of remembering, accompanying, benefiting, and preserving the people of Israel. Later in Acts, this salvation will extend also to non-Jews (gentiles) when they hear the gospel message and find full inclusion within the people of God. As the Holy Spirit, God continues to dwell among Jesus's followers and to constitute them as a people who share in God's emerging kingdom (Luke 22:29) in which "some are last who will be first, and some are first who will be last" (13:29–30).

The "promise" Peter speaks about therefore includes the arrival of *the Holy Spirit*, which Peter refers to in 2:33 as "the promise of the Holy Spirit." The Holy Spirit is the gift of God's own self, the life and presence of God come to dwell among humanity. In Acts, the Spirit presents an undeniable token or sign that God's salvation is present and real. The Spirit also brings the power inherent in that salvation, for the Spirit incorporates people into communities of faith, adding them as members of God's people, declaring them forgiven, and fostering communities that live out "saved" existence in their mutuality, unity, and charity.

Peter does not state it so simply, but the message of Pentecost—as the culmination of what Jesus's life, death, resurrection, and ascension set in motion—is this: God's salvation has arrived in its fullness. It has been made complete. It is certain. You can count on it, for the coming of God's Spirit means the promise has been kept. God has neither forgotten nor abandoned God's people.

Who are these people? Acts will expand this group in the chapters to come. As mentioned above regarding Peter's statement about the promise also being for "all who are far away," the book leans toward openness and expansion. The people reside out there. Others will join the offspring of Abraham and the ancient Israelites. Others will encounter God's salvation and learn that this God is trustworthy.

This outward-looking vision, anchored in the continuity between the newly given Spirit, Jesus, and God's old promises to make and preserve a people, raises expectations for God's salvation to leave its mark on the world. This salvation's fullness remains an unfolding fullness. At this early juncture in Acts, no one has an idea of exactly what it might look like for God's promises to draw in and transform "all who are far away." Still, the question is raised: What if God really means it? *Who* from far away might show up?

By the time the book is done, readers will have a clearer if not complete sense of what Peter's words really mean. God's promises will extend to people residing in places both familiar and exotic. The circles will widen, and some of the presumed terms by which people join and live as the people of God will change. Jesus's work in Acts by no means concludes with his ascension and the sending of the Holy Spirit. Yes, this work has kept promises about God's salvation, but Jesus still must flesh those out for us as we grow to understand better what kind of inclusion, renewal, and preservation God intends to accomplish, both in the pages of Acts and beyond. All this will prove disruptive to many people's assumptions.

When that happens, no one can say Peter didn't warn us.

Road Map

Emerging Realities

It's difficult to get a sense for how much time passes between Pentecost (Acts 2) and the death of Stephen (Acts 7). The narrative moves briskly, but many developments emerge in these chapters in which all the action occurs in Jerusalem.

Opposition arises. While our exploration will not dig deeply into the relevant verses, nevertheless we will note that the leaders of the Jerusalem temple arrest and interrogate apostles twice in Acts 4–5. The conflict offers an early indication that Acts will be a story of opposition and struggle as much as one of growth and inclusion. It's a disruptive gospel.

At the same time, the community of Jesus's followers thrives. These early chapters offer a nearly idealized portrait of the apostles' activities. Their preaching brings huge numbers of people into the fold. The authorities' threats appear to pose little risk. All of that will change when Stephen finds himself facing an angry mob at the end of Acts 6, but for now Acts depicts the initial response to the gospel among Jewish audiences in Jerusalem as very positive, just as in Luke 1–3 John's and Jesus's births were celebrated and John's ministry drew crowds. We will examine a few growing pains in the following chapters, but they come within a wider context of enthusiasm and vitality.

One important, foundational theme of Acts 2–7 comes in the narrative's references to the salvation God provides through Jesus. Previous chapters in this book have already mentioned salvation language in Peter's Pentecost sermon; it's language Peter uses without explanation, both in that sermon and in others to come. Acts refrains from clearly defining salvation. The book prefers to paint a picture over spelling out a formula. Keep a lookout for all the things God promises and does to benefit people, according to Acts. Taken together, those things constitute a broad salvation.

Some Christians speak of "being saved" as experiencing the forgiveness of their sins. There's more to salvation in Acts than this. Salvation in this book, as in the Gospel of Luke, certainly includes forgiveness (understood as being delivered here and now from sins, their dehumanizing burdens, and their negative practical consequences), but it encompasses other benefits too. Depending on the audience in a particular scene, salvation may entail healing, restoration to community (or new inclusion and belonging in community), and deliverance from idolatry (14:11–18), ignorance (17:29–31), or captivity to Satan (26:17–18). When God remembers God's people and comes to be with them to preserve them through Jesus's actions and the presence of the Holy Spirit, that's salvation. It's belonging. When God makes it so these people will always belong, so they can have a future with God that is unthreatened by death itself because of the resurrection of Jesus, that also is salvation. Salvation means not being left alone or relinquished as prey to oppressive forces, whether those are spiritual influences, dehumanizing ailments, overbearing empires, cycles of subjugation to unjust policies and people, death, or our own sheer ignorance. By disrupting all these things, by targeting them for destruction even through enduring their violence, God saves.

Acts speaks about salvation not to enumerate everything God does on humanity's behalf but to extol the God who accomplishes that salvation. Consider the kind of God who is *implied* by all the action and promises recounted in Acts, particularly in the forthcoming chapters: in the preaching, in the book's descriptions of community life, and in the ways Jesus's followers deal with obstacles. A God who heals, restores, and delivers must be merciful and generous. A God who can save must be stronger than the forces that endanger. A God who establishes a people and dwells among them must be faithful to keep promises and also powerful enough to see them through.

The next few chapters will help us see in what ways those claims might be true and how the people of God might experience them.

Acts 3:11–26 and 4:5–12

The Ultimate Disruption

The God of our ancestors has glorified his servant Jesus,
whom you handed over and rejected. (Acts 3:13)

The early chapters of Acts devote considerable attention to sermons
about Jesus Christ. Through these sermons, Acts enlarges its portrait
of the God who brings salvation through Jesus, underscoring God's
commitment to accomplish certain ends and prodding us to consider
the roles Jesus's followers play as God demonstrates this commitment.

As the earlier chapters exploring Acts 2 indicated, the sermons
emphasize Jesus as the fulfillment of God's promises. Through Jesus's life, death, resurrection, and ascension God makes salvation
available, bringing those who repent—who recognize God at work
in Jesus—into the fellowship of God's people by empowering them
with the Holy Spirit and preserving them for a future with God.

Peter's speeches in Acts 3 and 4 continue to speak about Jesus as the
decisive means by which God accomplishes God's purposes. Anyone
who demands clear explanations of exactly *how* God brings about
new realities through Jesus, or exactly *why* Jesus's life, death, and
resurrection had to transpire for the Holy Spirit to come, will come
away from these chapters disappointed. The recurring insistence is
instead *that* Jesus brings about the fulfillment of God's design as
Israel's promised Messiah. Peter cannot prove that Jesus brings God's

intentions to fruition, but he does seek to demonstrate that the time of fruition has indeed arrived.

Peter's words in these chapters follow a miraculous event in the Jerusalem temple: Peter heals a man who cannot walk "in the name of Jesus Christ" (3:1–10; see also 4:10). Summoning Jesus's name means Peter calls upon Jesus's power. He presents himself as a mediator, one who wields Jesus's authority for the sake of accomplishing Jesus's purposes. Peter claims no special power for himself but participates in Jesus's ongoing ministry of compassion and relief. By bringing a man to "perfect health" and thereby perhaps providing him with a way out of his related conditions of poverty and disability, Peter claims that Jesus, "the Author of life" (3:15), saves people from whatever afflicts them. Like in the Gospel according to Luke, salvation means restoration; it encompasses all facets of human need, treating physical, social, and spiritual well-being as an integrated whole.

As he speaks about this "Author of life" and the salvation now available, Peter's speeches concentrate on at least four topics.

First, Jesus's death exposes humanity's ignorance, and his resurrection vindicates him and his claims. Peter's sermons indict his audience as Jesus's killers (2:23, 36; 3:13–15), even though these crowds were not the ones who actually ordered, conducted, or necessarily supported the crucifixion. They nevertheless bear responsibility in a corporate way, for they belong to the masses who have not (yet) recognized Jesus as the Messiah sent by God. Their ignorance may have been understandable once (3:17), but it no longer has an excuse in the aftermath of the resurrection, which Peter describes as an act of God. This message recurs throughout Acts 2–4: you killed Jesus, but God raised him from the dead (2:23–24, 36; 3:15; 4:10; see also 5:30). God broke in, Peter says, upending humanity's ignorance and hostility with a clear vindication of Jesus and a durable display of power over death. In the resurrection, God declares Jesus is Messiah; God's ways cannot be thwarted even by people's rejection of this Messiah—nor even by death. The resurrection stands, then, as a statement of God's ultimate ability to disrupt the way things are and presumably the way things always have to be. Although we thought death was final, even it proves no obstacle to God's commitments to be known, to persist despite opposition, and to reorder human existence.

Second, Peter contends that God's raising Jesus from the dead was not Plan B. The resurrection was not a case of God fixing something that went wrong; instead, it was part of what God intended to do all along. In 3:18, Peter refers to what God "foretold." Similarly, back in 2:23, Peter described Jesus's arrest and prosecution "according to the definite plan and foreknowledge of God" (see also 4:24–28). Curiously, however, even though Jesus's death was part of this plan, still Peter castigates his Jerusalem audiences for their responsibility in the crucifixion, probably because they represent the overall populace of Jerusalem, where Jesus suffered rejection (see Luke 13:33–34; 19:41–44). How can Peter have it both ways? Did God orchestrate everything according to plan, or did people choose to reject and eliminate the Messiah? Acts seems unconcerned about finding a problem with or taking sides in a debate that keeps students in Introduction to Philosophy courses awake at night: whether people's actions are predetermined or we have freedom to make our own decisions.

In ways that Acts never clearly explains, somehow Jesus's death and resurrection fulfill or manifest a divine design; they accomplish what God wills (see Luke 22:42; Acts 4:27–28). Yet Peter also holds people responsible for Jesus's execution even as he condemns and shakes his head at the folly of their attempts to resist what God determined to accomplish through Jesus.

We should not read too much into references to God's plan in Acts. Some have, alas, done exactly that, spinning theories about a universe in which God has already dictated everything that will ever occur, including what I will eat for lunch next Thursday. These beliefs quickly run aground when we ponder why God might predetermine so many messed-up aspects of our universe, or what kind of God might decide that a certain child "must" get leukemia. In the end, they can paint God as capricious and suggest we excuse history's atrocities because they serve some greater, invisible good.

Those theories of an all-powerful Puppet Master belong more to films such as *The Adjustment Bureau* than to the Bible. True, some biblical texts speak of God's activity on display in historical events, but just as many describe God's vulnerability to all that occurs in the world. It's a mixed message. When Acts speaks about God's plan, we should understand this as referring to what God *is determined* to do, not what God *has* to do to follow some preordained cosmic blueprint. Whether the author of Acts believed that history proceeds according to an elaborate script, we may never know. I find it much more plausible to consider "the definite plan . . . of God" as referring, rather, to God's dedication to seeing some things through, no matter what forces may try to thwart God's commitments through ignorance or malice. God's plan, then, includes bringing salvation. It includes the eventual defeat of evil. It means God will follow through on pledges, even if setbacks and oppositions will inevitably occur. It does not mean God decreed long ago that I will get a good parking space at the mall and you will not.

Third, now that God has made salvation available through Jesus and the coming of the Holy Spirit, what happens next? Acts has little to say in explicit terms about a coming end of history or Jesus's future return. It focuses instead on the present tense and God's presence in the work of those who currently bear witness to salvation. The present resides between Pentecost and the expected "time of universal restoration" (3:21) in which all of God's intentions will find fulfillment and the reign of God announced and embodied in Jesus's ministry will bring health and wholeness to all aspects of human existence. The preaching in Acts does not threaten future punishment or suffering for nonbelievers; the negative outcome mentioned in the sermons is the prospect of nonparticipation in the people of God and in the blessings they enjoy (3:23, blending words from Deuteronomy 18:19–20 and Leviticus 23:29).

The current time in the history of God's salvation is an era of repentance, mentioned in 2:38 and again in 3:19 (see also 5:31). *Repentance*, as discussed previously, refers to recognizing God's activity on humanity's behalf, specifically, activity manifested in Jesus Christ. The whole of Acts tells of Jesus's followers trying to bring others (who, taken together, represent "all the families of the earth" according to Acts 3:25, reprising parts of Genesis 22:18 and 26:4) to this point of recognition, so they might find themselves included in the communities that celebrate and express God's salvation. As a result, Acts is much less a book about what God will do someday than it is an appeal to begin discovering God's presence and living in light of God's promised benefits right now.

The communities that form in Acts take on crucial importance for understanding what it means to discover God. Even though it can be easy to overlook the communities because of the heavy attention the narrative gives to Peter, Paul, and others who occupy the limelight, these individual speakers all represent larger groups. And Jesus resides among these groups. This leads to the fourth point about the book's early sermons: they raise the question of Jesus's current location. Peter says in 3:21 that Jesus will "remain in heaven" until God restores all things. Other parts of Acts describe Jesus likewise, as beside God (Acts 2:33–34). Jesus is somewhere else, absent from the earth. Or is he?

He both is and is not. Jesus remains present in the world through the presence of the Holy Spirit, whom he himself sends to all his people (2:33) and who is, according to 16:7, "the Spirit of Jesus." Jesus's followers repeatedly refer to "the name of Jesus" or "the name of the Lord" in Acts. In this name, people are baptized, experience healing, and receive forgiveness. To act and speak in Jesus's name is to operate as his representatives. It is to identify with him by participating in communities that he creates and defines. In this way, Jesus's followers continue Jesus's ministry not just by doing the same things he once did but by operating under his influence and mediating his presence through words and deeds. Where is Jesus? Present in the life, worship, and ministry of his followers as well as in the places they will go.

The close associations Acts makes between Jesus's influence and the activities of his followers should make us less inclined to embrace a religious view in which God exists somewhere "out there" while we human beings hope to make an occasional connection. The Gospel of Luke characterizes Jesus's life as a prolonged "visitation" (see Luke 19:44). Acts implies the visitation continues; Jesus has settled in among humanity—still working, still saving. We can find him manifest in Christian communities. Or at least we are supposed to.

If Jesus's connection to his followers exists today in ways similar to what Acts suggests, then Acts encourages me to see churches (the people, not the buildings) as vital communities, crucial for the gospel of God's salvation to remain known and attractive for generations to come. This connection also raises cautionary red flags, given that many people have long catalogs of instances in which churches (the institutions *and* their members) have been abusive, selfish, or apathetic. Or simply boring. When Acts ties Jesus and his people together in such tight knots, its theological vision can spawn idealism or cynicism, depending on my perspective and how motivated I am to get out of bed on a given Sunday morning.

The communities of believers that spring into being in Acts exist as the products of some major disruptions: Jesus visited, he was resurrected, and the Holy Spirit came. The Christian communities that exist now have organic connections to those disruptive experiences from long ago. But smaller, less perceptible disruptions also hold these communities together. To see them, we need to peer deeply into these groups and consider the individuals who compose them. What troubles, determinations, or longings make a person participate in a community of faith? What kind of salvation draws her in? How does she hope her involvement might affect the wider world? Ask these questions of enough Christians enough times, and we may begin to see signs of Jesus in the experiences of his followers even now.

Finally, God is not limited to the communities we encounter in Acts. Later in the story, further disruptions will come. Many of these shocks to the status quo will convince members of those communities that God is also busy elsewhere, accomplishing salvation and occasionally directing Jesus's followers to catch up and recognize other ways of doing things and other places to do them. These parts of Acts remind readers that the communities of Jesus's followers, although they are crucial means for people to experience salvation, are not exclusive or required means. God works in other settings too. The plan of God remains much grander, and more spread out.

It remains so today.

Acts 4:32–5:11

Communal Harmony
as a Matter of Life or Death

Now the whole group of those who believed were of one
heart and soul. (Acts 4:32)

Two scenes: the first paints perhaps the most attractive picture in all of
Acts; the second, the most repellent. The first describes how believers
in Jerusalem share their wealth and selflessly care for one another's
needs. The second tells of two members of this community who try
to defraud the group and fall down dead as a result. Generosity and
trust in the first exceed our wildest dreams for what seems possible.
Stiff (and, it seems, divinely ordained!) punishments greatly surpass
the crime's severity in the second.

The scenes belong together as a contrasting pair of snapshots. Both
involve sold property and proceeds placed at the apostles' feet, and
both include evidence of God's activity. Both are important pieces in
the book's overall depiction of believers in community.

The first scene, in Acts 4:32–37, resumes a description from Acts
2:43–47, when the coming of the Holy Spirit on the day of Pentecost led to the creation of a tightly knit community in Jerusalem.
This unified and growing community, we learned in that previous
account, spends its time engaged in worship, fellowship, and charity.

The portrait of mutuality sparkles: truly cooperative living is fueled by intense generosity and marked by worship and service. At the end of Acts 4, the focus zeroes in on a particular aspect of the group's behavior: members who own property and homes sell them and present the apostles with the proceeds. By laying piles of money at their leaders' feet, the donors acknowledge the apostles' authority to distribute the wealth as needed, according to what meets others' needs. As a result, "not a needy person" can be found in the group. It sounds like a promise God made to the ancient Hebrews after delivering them from slavery and guiding them to the promised land: "There will, however, be no one in need among you, because the LORD is sure to bless you" (Deuteronomy 15:4).

If this image of a generous community possessing "one heart and soul" sounds appealing to us, it also surely tickled the ears of an ancient audience. The ethos described here resembles the descriptions of authentic friendship in a handful of ancient Greek philosophical writings. Some of those texts described a state of affairs like this as what could be possible under ideal social and political systems. Other, more propagandistic traditions associated ideals about shared possessions with a golden age of civil harmony rooted in what Emperor Augustus set in motion in establishing the Roman Empire. As Acts describes the believers in Jerusalem, however, their mutuality springs into being not through the right political architecture but through the work of the Holy Spirit. The community God creates displays a capacity for realizing deep, nearly unrealistic hopes for justice, generosity, and coexistence. God's presence manifests itself in the "great power" (see Luke 24:49; Acts 1:8) at work in the apostles' ministry and in the unity, formed by "great grace," that is the community's hallmark. The passage does not celebrate this fellowship for its own sake; it celebrates the community as a place where God's salvation can be experienced.

As we have seen already, in Acts God exhibits an interest in reordering or restoring all aspects of human existence. This passage broadens our understanding of God's salvation, showing the gospel's implications for matters of wealth and social status. Giving to the needy does not earn salvation, but it demonstrates that a person has come to grasp what the economy of salvation is all about: relinquishing one's real and perceived advantages and entering into true solidarity with others. When Jesus was among the apostles in the Gospel of Luke, he envisioned a similar kind of discipleship, one so challenging it can strike fear.

> Lend, expecting nothing in return. (Luke 6:35)

> Sell your possessions, and give alms. Make purses for yourselves that do not wear out, an unfailing treasure in heaven, where no thief comes near and no moth destroys. For where your treasure is, there your heart will be also. (Luke 12:33–34)

> None of you can become my disciple if you do not give up all your possessions. (Luke 14:33)

> Sell all that you own and distribute the money to the poor, and you will have treasure in heaven; then come, follow me. (Luke 18:22)

When Barnabas and other believers in Jerusalem share their resources to support their outreach and to sustain the needy, they give evidence—or bear witness to the fact—that they live in light of God's intentions and Jesus's pattern for discipleship. They understand their united existence, sharing a single "heart and soul," as so tight that radical sharing of possessions seems a natural outgrowth. Their willingness to sell property to benefit others contrasts sharply with the greed of Judas Iscariot, who used the money he received for delivering up Jesus to purchase property for his own benefit, showing where his heart resided (Acts 1:18–19).

But then, in the second scene, Acts offers another disturbing contrast to Barnabas and friends. First Ananias, then his wife, Sapphira, fall down dead at Peter's feet after lies they tell come into view. Acts does not clearly indicate that Peter determines their horrible fate; their sin is not against him, and so he appears as more the messenger. Nor do they die from shock or some other strange coincidence. Does God kill them? That seems to be the implication. What kind of God does this, and why?

The story elicits a range of emotions: amazement, anger, and fear. The narrative, with its suspense and repetition, seems to want to be funny here, at least for those who appreciate gallows humor. But it can be difficult to laugh when death, and not a pie in the face, punishes those who misreport their income. And when God, supposedly a merciful God, apparently ordains the punishment. And when the guilty are afforded no opportunity to repent or make restitution once their lies come to the surface.

This story cannot finally be tamed. That is, it will always retain some of its moral offense because the punishments do not fit the transgression. It makes God out to be, well, excessive. Isn't God more than a petty moralistic police officer? Other biblical passages give us good reason to doubt God is like this. (And certainly some additional passages suggest this is precisely who God is!) In any case, this one will always remain on short lists of "stories many of us would like to remove from the Bible." This does not mean it cannot teach us if we look more closely, however.

The conversations Ananias and Sapphira have with Peter indicate that selling property and donating the proceeds is not necessarily a requirement for joining the community of faith. Peter reminds Ananias that the land and the money were his to do with as he wished. The couple's misstep instead lies in misrepresenting their donation as the property's full sale price. Legally speaking, the land likely belongs to Ananias as head of a household; in 5:4 Peter speaks of the unsold land and the proceeds as only *his* (each "your" and "you" in this verse is singular in the original Greek). Sapphira's offense consists of being a willing conspirator and covering for her husband. Just a portion of the proceeds could have been a welcome gift to the community. Their sin is deceit; they ultimately defraud God, not the people who receive the donation.

Peter's claim about lying to God should make us pause. How is an attempt to deceive the community tantamount to trying to deceive God or testing God? Peter does not claim to be God, but he does point to the community's importance in God's eyes. The community, therefore, somehow expresses God's own self, God's own intentions. How does it do this? Through its unity and mutuality. Holding back money is not the problem; the problem is creating a false impression of commitment to the community and to God's purposes. Ananias and Sapphira, compelled by what Peter identifies as a satanic impulse in Ananias's heart, perpetrate a lie about themselves and their commitment to the community's well-being. This goes beyond simple hypocrisy, for they hold back their selves. They demonstrate contempt for the community's purpose not as an economic experiment but as an expression of radical commitment to one's neighbors. Because this unified community that God has been constructing since Pentecost stands as a living articulation of what God intends the gospel to accomplish, showing disdain for it and its ethos makes the lie's motive "satanic."

If this passage provokes questions about "what kind of God" might kill Ananias and Sapphira or expect us to laugh at their demise, it also makes us wonder, what kind of community is this that God so vigorously protects? A detail at the very end might help us think about this.

In 5:11 we read, "And great fear seized the whole church and all who heard of these things." No surprise there. But notice the word *church*. That word has not yet appeared in this discussion, nor previously in my descriptions of the activity recounted in Acts 1–4, because the word does not appear in Acts (or in the Gospel of Luke, for that matter) until this precise moment in the story. The "group of those who believed" has shown itself so far in Acts to be capable of great things. In 5:1–11, we see also its capacity for self-destructive behavior. It's almost as if we have to see the best and the worst in this community before it gets called "the church."

Can this church hope to survive all the bad behavior and half-hearted commitments of its members? Is God going to have to knock all of them down dead? Is the point of the story that people inside and outside the church should look upon the church and its struggles and come away with great fear?

We know there must be more to it than this. Obviously God's normal practice does not involve policing the church in such horrific ways. This is a good thing. Because if God were really like this, not many of us would remain; most of us would quickly give up on such a trigger-happy God, while the rest would get zapped within a week or two.

Why does Acts find Ananias and Sapphira's story worth telling? Who clings to such a story, with its image of a quick-tempered, no-second-chances-for-you God? Who thinks or hopes that God acts in such a way? Maybe angry people do. Or threatened people. Or fearful people. Not people suffering from merely any kind of fear—maybe these particular people fear losing what is truly life-giving to them. Maybe the passage comes from people afraid of losing a community capable of embodying the best things, such as God's very own commitment to them. Those people might fear losing hope for what God can make possible for them, their loved ones, and their neighbors in need. If fear stalks this passage and the path it took to get into the New Testament, perhaps this fierce and vengeful fear nevertheless exposes how important the beautiful parts of this passage are and how desperately we long to experience community and flourishing like what we read about at the end of Acts 4. The passage reminds us how difficult it is to create such a place, given all our flaws and suspicions. When something comes along to make our difficult lives easier or more pleasant, we achingly want God to protect it, sometimes at any cost.

The history of the church suggests that "the church" will always contain both self-giving and false commitment to others, as well as everything in between. As I look across my own life, I have found within the church—both congregations and Christian communities of various kinds—incredible generosity. I mean more than financial generosity: authentic, radical acceptance of others. I have received compassionate support during personal tragedies. And yet I have also encountered in the church some of the most self-centered, destructive, manipulative behavior that I've ever seen anywhere in society. I have suffered from slander, exclusion, disappointment, and simple old-fashioned sociopathic behavior.

Then again, God only knows the extent to which I myself have damaged and let down others in the church.

I love the church. I hate the church. But for some reason, I just cannot leave it. Finally, I see in the church not just the best and the worst of humanity but the best and worst of myself. And God has not struck me down dead yet, so I think I will keep on being part of it, even though it will always include people I sometimes wish would fall down dead because of their crimes against Christian unity.

But what if God is *there*, in the mix of this flawed and occasionally self-destructive body of people called the church? That is a fearful, mysterious thought.

It would be shortsighted to read this passage and assume its message is "Look out! God is really vindictive!" Instead, the severe consequences for Ananias and Sapphira announce, "Look out! This new, splendid community is quite vulnerable. Don't hurt it!" Although the church has been brought into existence by God's own Spirit, it remains at risk of being undone by the deceit of its own members.

In the end, then, this story is less about the right use of wealth and property than it is about God's commitment to preserve the church. Despite its irredeemable features, this passage suggests that God is so deeply woven into the fabric of the church, or the church is so deeply woven into the life of God, that the church's existence and unity remain somehow essential. In this way, the community (any community) of believers can be considered holy ground. God's commitment to the church remains resolute even in spite of its members' occasional bad behavior. The unity, vitality, witness, and even fragility of these communities are part of encountering God in their midst.

Unity is difficult; sometimes it appears impossible. But it is also a foundational goal if Christians, despite our many flaws, are going to be able to give voice to God's presence in and on behalf of the world.

Acts 6:1–7

Growth Brings Change—
and Surprise

The word of God continued to spread. (Acts 6:7)

No one ever said this would be easy.

Many kinds of threats beset Jesus's followers and their communities in Acts. Some of these stem from internal deceit (recall Ananias and Sapphira in Acts 5:1–11 and the mention of Satan filling Ananias's heart), while others arise from external opposition (which increases in Acts 5:17–42). On the whole, Acts gives about as much attention to the church's endangerments as to its progress or successes. In this passage, the church's existence and effectiveness remain vulnerable—not to problems brought to it but to problems developing more organically. Indeed, the issue addressed here appears to stem partially from the church's own vigor and growth.

The problem concerns a dispute between two groups within the Jerusalem church. Imagine that—one group of Christians complaining about another! So much for romantic images of the earliest churches being harmonious and always at peace with themselves.

Acts names the groups: Hellenists and Hebrews. But we receive no explanation of what defines them. Scholars' best hypotheses conclude one group comprises Greek-speakers while the other one speaks

Hebrew or another Semitic dialect, probably Aramaic. Both groups are Jews who follow Jesus as Messiah; the problems that arise relate to their cultural and linguistic differences.

Sharing and communal meals contribute to the identity and reputation of this community (see Acts 2:44–47; 4:34), but a problem develops. Somehow, widows from the Hellenist group suffer neglect in the food distribution. What does this mean? Perhaps widows do not receive the food they need. Or perhaps widows who expect to play active roles in the distribution are being denied the opportunity to serve in this way. Or, maybe the stress relates to differences in dietary practices. Acts does not offer a definitive answer.

What may be only a logistical problem for a growing subculture of Jews from different regions cannot be treated as "simply" logistical because the wrinkles or offenses fall along ethnic or cultural lines. Clearly some perceive prejudice: the Hellenist widows suffer because they are Hellenists. It takes little imagination to understand how this might have developed or how it might have extremely negative consequences for the church's ability to thrive and bear witness to Jesus as a unified, just community. Truly the problem needs resolution, lest the church devolve into a collection of sniping factions.

The solution appears relatively straightforward, or at least uncomplicated to institute: the apostles (referred to as "the twelve") instruct "the whole community" to choose seven men to oversee the food distribution. They also set several criteria for guiding the selection but provide no explanation for why the number should be seven and why those appointed must all be men. Some readers see creative problem-solving here, while others see an attempt to take the job of the community's important food-service ministry away from women and to "institutionalize" it under male overseers. In any case, our ability to identify possible injustices in the apostles' criteria underscores the different ways in which communities must work hard to discern God's leading in decision making. Our decision making always reflects our theological values, how we understand God to be at work in the world and in its people. These values affect how we perceive problems when they arise as well as our assumptions about the solutions available to us. It makes good sense, then, to be clear about those values and to hold them up for regular scrutiny.

It is not clear who chooses the seven, but the instructions of the twelve suggest that "the whole community" picks them. The syntax in 6:6 also allows for the possibility that the whole community prays and lays hands on the seven to commission them. This decision involves the entire group; the leadership does not make it in a secluded back room or by means of private emails.

We learn very little about the seven. One, Nicolaus, is a gentile who converted to Judaism, which lessens the chance he speaks Hebrew and increases the likelihood he speaks Greek. All of them have Greek names, but this does not necessarily mean all are Hellenists. Still, their names may reflect sensitivity among the community that these new leaders should be trusted by or should share affinities with the slighted group of Hellenists.

Does this passage have anything to say about God? It looks mainly like an instance of disagreement and problem solving. After all, God does not command anyone to do anything, and no one claims to speak on God's behalf. If we compare this episode to all the others from Acts treated thus far in this book, God appears rather absent or irrelevant to the situation at hand. Yes, Acts emphasizes the presence of the Holy Spirit in the seven men as an important qualification of their suitability to do the task. But there are additional details we should note as well.

First, the apostles' decision to delegate the job of food distribution probably indicates their determination to focus their own energy on performing miraculous deeds and proclaiming the message about Jesus. At the same time, it raises questions about how much they understand the full extent of that message. Their words suggest that "to wait on tables" is to "neglect the word of God." Their point is understandable if they mean there is not enough time in the day to accomplish all that needs doing. And yet Jesus never told them that they should understand their role as evangelists as an exclusive responsibility. Others might help them in this work of furthering the word of God in public places (as indeed happens, a point I will return to very soon). Furthermore, the ministry of "the word of God" goes beyond preaching. It includes—you guessed it—waiting on tables.

Jesus himself indicated exactly as much in Luke 22:24–27, when he declared that a leader among his followers must be "like one who serves," even as Jesus himself related to his disciples "as one who serves." This expression, "one who serves," can also be translated, as it is in Acts 6:2, as one who "waits on tables." To serve food to others, as an expression of charity, care, and hospitality, is to imitate Jesus.

Second, if the apostles indeed mistakenly consider food service beneath their dignity, Acts does not dwell on it. At the same time, Acts does not devote much attention to the domestic duties performed by the seven men chosen by the community to do that work. Immediately after this passage concludes, Stephen, one of the seven, steps into the narrator's spotlight not because of his skill in serving tables but because of his growing renown for performing "wonders and signs among the people" and his wise speech that confounds his opponents—all very apostle-like activities, on the whole. These deeds hardly belong to the apostles alone. The irony leaps off the page: the church needs to coordinate its ministry of care; the church needs people to proclaim the word of God; organized leadership helps cover all the chores; but God's Spirit will nevertheless prod people to find themselves adequate and available for all kinds of tasks. God can and will accompany anyone. Food servers serve God in distributing food but also in proclaiming the good news. Organization helps the church, but the roles assigned by the organization hardly preclude God's ability to use people in a variety of ways, in a variety of settings.

Third, the conclusion of this passage confirms "Crisis averted!" when it reports, "The word of God continued to spread; the number of the disciples increased greatly in Jerusalem, and a great many of the priests became obedient to the faith." The Jerusalem church's numbers continue to increase, and—perhaps surprisingly, given the opposition the church faced from some members of the Jerusalem priesthood in preceding chapters—priests constitute a segment of the new membership. The church, having attended to disagreements within its own ranks, bears powerful witness to Jesus.

At the same time, Acts does not permit us to view the church's numerical growth as proof of its own faithfulness or cleverness. "The church" does not spread; "the word of God" is what expands. But this expansion involves more than geographical aspects; the point is:

the word of God gets bigger. In this instance, the meaning of "the word of God" extends beyond "the message of the gospel." Acts uses the expression to make it sound nearly synonymous with the church itself, the community of Jesus's many and diverse disciples. To join the church is to join the word. The word of God is not something the church bears or announces; the word of God is what the church *lives*, or *manifests*, in its life together and its outreach to the world. So closely bound is God to the church that the church's vitality is the vitality of God's word. The church is the expression of God's good news. This church, as we have seen, encompasses much more than the twelve apostles and their particular functions. The word of God contains multitudes.

Given the importance of the church for expressing God's word to its neighbors, no wonder it is so important that the dispute between the Hellenists and the Hebrews not erupt into something divisive or harmful. That would not necessarily hamper the church's effectiveness to do the work it is supposed to do. But it would undoubtedly hamper the church's ability to live authentically according to its identity. As previous chapters have indicated, Acts reminds us of how deeply God is intertwined in the life of the church. This is a rather audacious claim for us to hear, especially for those of us who are all too familiar with churches' shortcomings and prejudices.

The book of Acts has a penchant for making problem solving look rather simple. We all know that creating a task force of seven men will not solve every crisis that comes along. Acts does not provide a template or model for organizing the church or understanding how leadership works best. Different issues give rise to different solutions and different means of decision making. It would be a mistake to read this passage as just a statement about the apostles' importance or as merely an imperative for good church organization.

And yet, the story about the choosing of the seven says something about faithful ministry. The problem created by the neglect of Hellenist widows could escalate into a very serious one, or perhaps it gives indication of grave bias already existing in the community. Many of us instinctively respond to problems or threats of expanding disputes in our own communities as signs of failure or dysfunction. Yet the crisis described at the beginning of Acts 6 leads Jesus's followers to seek new, corrective ways forward, not to assign blame. The problem provides an opportunity for the community to reflect on its values and the work it has been charged to carry out. The most charitable way to describe their willingness to adjust their organizational structure is that they are open to discerning new ways of expressing their obedience to God and their commitments to one another. They willingly respond to the need for change. God may bless those efforts, as when "the word of God" gains new members, and God may also continue to work outside of the prescribed organizational structure by empowering some like Stephen to bear witness to the gospel in numerous ways.

Acts shows no embarrassment about Stephen's multifaceted ministry, a ministry that looks much like the apostles'. He reflects a church open to responding to God, open to adjusting its strategies to meet its changing circumstances, open to honoring its differences, and open to being surprised by the new opportunities God might create. The mission of the Jerusalem community extends beyond getting the job done, distributing food efficiently, or resolving internal conflict. It involves exercising leadership in ways that honor a God who will be found in a variety of locales—among widows gathering together in a private home for lunch, within the church's most public efforts to articulate the gospel, and all places in between. To honor this God is to open ourselves to encountering God both in the open and behind the scenes, to bear authentic witness in the midst of both harmony and dispute.

Acts 7:54–60

Using Violence to Keep God under Control

Lord, do not hold this sin against them. (Acts 7:60)

In case we forget, stories like this one quickly remind us: the Bible is a very violent book.

Biblical violence cuts in multiple directions, including senseless violence suffered by innocent people, state-sanctioned violence perpetrated to coerce or punish, or hopes for violent retribution to set the score straight. Some parts of the Bible speak of God using, promising, or permitting violence (recall, for example, the troubling deaths of Ananias and Sapphira in Acts 5:1–11). Other parts describe violence as a tool used by people to oppose God and God's ways.

Among passages in which God's people suffer violence, Stephen's death in Acts is a particularly nasty instance. While there is no pleasant way to be murdered, being pelted with rocks launched from the hands of people in your own community—perhaps people with whom you have worshiped or shared meals, people you recognize as you make momentary eye contact with them before their stones hit you in the face—strikes us as especially barbaric.

To understand why Stephen dies we need to consider what comes before, in Acts 6:8–7:53. His attention-catching ministry in Jerusalem arouses opposition from a group of fellow Jews who characterize his message, through the testimony of false witnesses they have put up to the task, as anti-Moses (and therefore hostile to the law of Moses) and anti-temple. Those who have read the Gospels may hear echoes of accusations against Jesus in Matthew and Mark (see, for example, Mark 14:56–59). Surely a point of Stephen's story is that Jesus's followers might expect no better treatment than Jesus himself received.

The rules did not change after the original Easter. Anyone who thinks that the resurrection of Jesus Christ reformed humanity or necessarily broke our cycles of violence learns otherwise from Stephen's death. The demise of James in Acts 12 reiterates the point, as do the hardships Paul and others will endure later in the story. Jesus's followers continue Jesus's ministry; so they also find themselves facing the opposition Jesus's ministry continues to provoke.

Stephen's death is as confident as it is vicious. Connections between Luke and Acts direct us to see the stoning of Stephen and the crucifixion of Jesus sharing a similar tone of gracious resolve: both men speak their last words crying out in a loud voice (Luke 23:46; Acts 7:60), yet both seek forgiveness for their killers (Luke 23:34; Acts 7:60). Because of Jesus's model, his followers can die with assurance. When Stephen dies with firm faith, calling on Jesus to receive his spirit, he brings Jesus's death into view again. Jesus, who recited Psalm 31:5 as he expired in Luke 23:46 ("Father, into your hands I commend my spirit"), also died in a trusting, exemplary manner.

Confidence abounds as the stones fly. One of the final things Stephen sees is a vision of the resurrected and exalted Jesus, "the Son of Man," who stands (not sits, presumably because he performs some kind of active role) at "the right hand of God" (indicating Jesus's unique honor and power). The vision means to reassure: the reality of Jesus's exaltation suggests God will vindicate faithful Stephen too. The vision also confirms the primary theological theme of Stephen's defense speech, a long retelling of Israel's history in 7:1–53 to the high priest and his council before they (and perhaps some allies with them) take up stones to bash his skull: God has never been and will never be confined to a particular place, such as a temple (Acts 7:48).

Themes of a roaming, accessible God run throughout Acts. Paul expresses them to a gentile audience in Athens in 17:24–29. God's

Spirit, freely moving out into the world in the pages of Acts, directs Jesus's followers and ensures the spread of God's word, the message and power of the gospel. Communities of faith encounter God and express God's desires in their corporate worship, sharing, and service. Stephen's death, while grisly and tragic, is part of a larger narrative determined to confirm that the realities of God's presence and promises are not imperiled by the hostility that may greet and destroy those who announce such things.

Despite Stephen's poise and faith, still Acts does not put too happy a face on his dying. Nothing suggests that death purifies him, anyone else, or the wider church. His demise is not necessary; no one in Acts celebrates it. Even though it sparks widespread persecution in Acts 8, persecution that drives most of Jesus's followers out of Jerusalem and ends up promoting the spread of the gospel, still it's ugly. It's a loss.

Stephen's death appears as a landmark and a token of judgment issued against his opponents, who come across as God's opponents. Acts keeps an eye on those who challenge the gospel, frequently chastising the violence perpetrated by the Jewish high priest and his closest advisers. This is the same collection of people who pursued a case against Jesus in Luke's Gospel and who will repeatedly try to destroy Paul in the last quarter of Acts. Sometimes their allies are groups who zealously defend the temple and the law of Moses, such as the people who oppose Stephen in Acts 6:9–10. Acts condemns them as God's enemies as much as it commends Jesus's followers as God's trustworthy servants.

But we can fall into a trap if we are not careful with how we read this neat division in the book's descriptions of the villains harassing the heroes.

The trap springs on us when we presume that the gospel creates Stephens and nothing else. The trap comes with assuming that we, those who seek to follow Jesus today, are always the righteous victims who need to be alert for some group of "others" out there waiting to oppress us in response to our faith commitments.

The trap also lurks in our inability to imagine how this passage warns us about our propensity to participate in violence as aggressors bent on furthering our own religious convictions. Stephen, after all, appears very much on the offensive too. Not to blame the victim for what happens, but Stephen's speech to his antagonists shows no desire for constructive dialogue. Acts may be guilty of boasting about him as an archetype for fiery instigators. Some have taken Stephen as a victim who gives them, in a twisted logic, license to act belligerently.

Christians are, because of their faith and practices, sometimes victims. We know that from Acts, occasional periods in history, and even news reports from around the globe in the twenty-first century. (It bears noting that religious persecution exists today as a real and increasingly common threat for many in the world who seek to live as Christians. Western Christians, who remain almost entirely immune from these threats, need not feel guilty about living within social fabrics knit from tolerance. Those fortunate enough to live in them should celebrate some societies' commitments to eliminating religious persecution for all, a civil value about which the people in the New Testament could not have dreamed. But we cannot let the absence of real, targeted persecution leave us unaware of or indifferent to the struggles others face.) At the same time, Christians, drawing motivation from their faith and practices, sometimes are perpetrators of violence. The story of Stephen's death should keep us watchful on all sides.

The people who batter Stephen's body are not local thugs. They do not represent foreign threats like the Roman soldiers who nailed Jesus to a cross. They are, at least from all appearances, upstanding religious folk: regular members of synagogues, committed leaders, religious professionals, and priests. They are guardians of valued traditions. They have, as the saying goes, skin in the game, because they have invested much of themselves in religious ideas and systems that they believe are vital for making God known in the world.

Why would decent religious people like *that*, let alone anyone else, stoop to violence to protect what they value?

For one reason, because their traditions—which are also our traditions—purport to license such activity. This is hardly the only stoning that the Bible describes. Parts of the Old Testament prescribe stonings, reminding horrified readers today of the need to read the Bible carefully and critically, always cognizant of the circumstances and conflicts out of which Scripture emerged. Judaism and Christianity, like other religious traditions, must contend with sacred texts that appear to endorse violent means of policing the insiders and punishing the outsiders. Religious issues and debates (like nonreligious ones) are never immune from inclinations to use the stick when the carrot does not work. "Having Jesus" has not prevented Christians from threatening and coercing others.

For another reason, the religious leaders who kill Stephen have, we might assume, allowed their responsibility to protect their understanding of God to become so pressing to them that it eclipses their ability to be curious about that understanding. That is, they cannot engage Stephen in authentic conversation about God because they (perhaps like him) have religious commitments that they will not permit to budge, commitments they will protect to the hilt before they consider other ways of understanding God. Their commitments might extend to presuming they know exactly how God works, and therefore they refuse to make room for anything a professed visionary like Stephen might say. They lash out in violence because they have fallen victim to the oldest sin in the book, idolatry.

Idolatry worships a creation instead of the Creator. Idolatry loves symbols more than the thing to which a symbol points. Idolatry satisfies itself with knockoffs and shadows. Idolatry imagines God can be contained and therefore controlled and owned. Because idolaters think they know where the treasure resides, they allow no alterations to their maps and they punish explorers—with violence, if necessary.

Stephen's speech to the high priest warns about idolatry when it re-proclaims (following Isaiah 66:1–2) God's dwelling as encompassing all of heaven and earth, not limited to a temple on a hill. He does not say the temple in Jerusalem is inherently idolatrous but implies that some—including a core group in his audience—have come to treat it in an idolatrous manner, giving it outsized importance and becoming unable to glimpse other places and ways where God has promised to be present.

The idolatry perverting Stephen's foes hardly afflicts them alone. It connects to more than high regard for temples and rightly interpreting the law of Moses. It involves temptations that beset probably all religious people (including Stephen?): to turn a quest for God into an enterprise of self-assured arrogance instead of a search requiring humble reliance on fellow seekers and openness to new and old ways of finding God. Stephen's story is not about rightly identifying and vilifying the bad guys. It's about coming to terms with the reality that all of us are too prone to reject God's messengers and cling ferociously to what we already know, or think we know, very well.

The antidote to idolatry is not to avoid being religious. Violence and self-assurance are hardly limited to religious people. It is not to withhold passion or conviction from our beliefs, nor to distrust all we think we know or can know about God. The answer involves keeping in view the object of our convictions—the possibility of encountering God. It likewise involves vigilantly noticing how our pursuing and safeguarding of these convictions leads us to deal with differences and dissent. If our convictions leave broken bodies in their wake, or if our pursuits of our religious values and prerogatives snuff out people's vitality in other ways, then we're almost certainly doing something wrong.

Fortunately, Acts, through its many connections to the Gospel of Luke, keeps our attention on Jesus's example. Not a high-octane Messiah but one willing to risk vulnerability, this Savior knows these dynamics of aggression and coercion up close, having suffered from them himself. Because of this, or perhaps despite it, he nevertheless remains committed to delivering us from our worst proclivities—even from our very violent selves.

Road Map

Expansions

Often in Acts a single event sets the story on a different trajectory. Obviously, the resurrection of Jesus was like that, setting all reality on a new course and making the story of Acts even needful or possible in the first place. These events and their resulting trajectories have theological dimensions, such as when people realize that *God* intends for gentiles, non-Jews, to hear about and freely receive salvation too. Acts shows an interest in geographical dimensions, as well, for the initiation of new trajectories sometimes re-aims the narrative's spotlight to follow characters into new locations. This begins in earnest in Acts 8, when persecution in Jerusalem causes many to flee.

Having fled, what will they do next? They will embody the gospel. They will bear witness to Jesus. Didn't he say to his followers in 1:8, "You will be my witnesses"?

But it isn't that self-evident. Although Jesus gave them a mission statement of sorts in 1:8, he didn't give them much in terms of specific guidance—neither in Acts nor throughout the Gospel according to Luke. As a result, there's surprise when the scope of the church's work expands in Acts 8–12. The only reason we're able to pause here and consult a narrative road map is that the whole terrain has already been mapped. We possess the story through Acts 28; we can see where the story goes, which helps us make better sense of what's going on at this point. The characters in these chapters don't get to read ahead.

The scenes in Acts 8–12 offer some of the most exciting, nearly rollicking material in all of Acts. People from Samaria believe the message about God's salvation and join the community of Jesus's followers. So too does a royal official returning home to Ethiopia. The church's avowed archenemy changes his mind, with the help of a hesitant disciple, and switches sides. A dead woman returns to life. A gentile Roman soldier, a centurion, not only receives the Holy Spirit but shares hospitality with his Jewish guests who tell him about Jesus. Then God humiliates a king named Herod, a man bent on killing church leaders. It feels rather exhausting and otherworldly, especially since miracles or extraordinary events figure in all these major scenes of growth, persistence, and expansion.

In the coming chapters, consider the implications of the expansion. Acts does not necessarily view the church from a bigger-is-better perspective. Instead, the mentality is this: God's salvation was prepared for the benefit of the whole world, and so God eagerly desires for it to influence the whole world.

Along with the flashy stories we will examine, this part of Acts also includes several short summaries to indicate the spread of the word of God (8:25, 40; 11:19–21). These summaries don't mention miraculous activity. They merely describe otherwise ordinary people interacting with those around them. This looks more like the life of faith I'm familiar with: nothing is especially dramatic; it's just about everyday faithfulness. Furthermore, in these chapters the church's energy isn't focused outward alone; all the while, established communities receive attention too as their members tend to one another's needs and promote the vibrancy of their life together (9:31; 11:25–30).

Also consider the challenges on display in these chapters. How do people know where to go and the right thing to do? Acts lays heavy emphasis on supernatural guidance, dissuading us from crediting human cleverness, wise strategizing, or good fortune for all the expansion. In these scenes, people spy unforeseen possibilities coming into view (Can we be united with *Samaritans*? I can't receive hospitality in a *gentile's* home, can I?), and Acts insists these developments are consonant with the gospel and are expressions of God's intentions. More than geography, what's really expanding is people's sense of salvation's wide reach. When that expansion occurs, Acts says, you can expect God to be present and God to become known.

We know from real life that salvation's reach doesn't always involve the whole world charting a new trajectory. Can Acts apply to our lives on a smaller scale? What about when salvation feels elusive and harder to experience? For some, just one more day of inner peace, sobriety, or reprieve from fear would be all the miracle they need—or can handle—today. Consider how Acts encourages us to look for the possibility of God quietly intruding into those places too.

Acts 8:4–25

Spiritual Power, Spiritual Gift, and Spiritual Greed

He . . . was amazed when he saw the signs and great miracles that took place. (Acts 8:13)

All throughout Acts 8 and into the following chapters, the church is on the move and continues to grow. What makes this happen? Acts usually describes God as having a hand in things. Anyone who thinks people hold all the power over the good news and God's gifts misunderstands the real story.

Still, other factors deserve some credit. Persecution compels Jesus's followers to venture outward. Nothing suggests God's hand guides the persecutors. The circumstances and accidents of history propel the church into new settings. When it gets there, God does not get left behind. God's commitment to see ministry done and to have salvation offered does not get derailed.

Prior to Acts 8, all the action occurs in Jerusalem or its environs. Although Jesus informed his followers in 1:8 that they would be his witnesses in the region of Judea, northward into Samaria, and indeed to "the ends of the earth," no one seems to have bought a map or browsed travel brochures. The change in locales comes with the death of Stephen at the end of Acts 7, since this event triggered "a severe persecution" in Jerusalem, which caused "all except the apostles" to hightail it into Judea and Samaria (8:1).

As a result, beginning with this passage new ministry happens in a variety of places; the scattered believers proclaim the word of God. Still, the narrative tracks only Philip for now. Acts does not try to tell the whole tale of the church's beginnings and growth. It tells selected stories meant to illustrate God's involvement in the church's life and the nature of the gospel the church proclaims.

Chances are, most of these dispersed members of the Christian community would have preferred to land in Judea instead of Samaria. The rocky character of the relationship between Samaritans and Jews who resided in both Galilee (north of Samaria) and Judea (to the south) often shows itself in the pages of the Gospels, but those books never explain it, assuming readers know the history of the bad blood. From the perspective of most first-century Galilean and Judean Jews (and, therefore, perhaps most of Jesus's followers), Samaritans were undesirable types. While both groups worshiped the God of Abraham, Isaac, and Jacob, the Samaritans were viewed by their neighbors to the north and south as the offspring of unfaithful Hebrews who had polluted their genealogies by marrying members of other nations. Each group had its own scriptural books, its own separate temple, and its own confidence that it represented the true lineage of Abraham's offspring. Each group considered itself God's uniquely chosen people. The resentment was religious, ethnic, national, and sometimes personal—also usually mutual.

Remarkably, however, when Acts turns to follow Philip, one of the seven selected to supervise food distribution in 6:1–6, we detect no hint of reluctance. The narrative mostly treats Samaria as any other place, not the abode of enemies. Philip enters a city (probably Sebaste or Shechem), preaches about Jesus as God's Messiah, performs signs and wonders, and oversees the baptism of crowds of men and women who believe what he says. He does the kinds of things previously performed in Acts by apostles (and by his colleague Stephen in 6:8–10), indicating once again that evangelism and other public ministry are not the exclusive domain of a rarefied few.

The narrator's summary proceeds briskly. Everything appears rather uncomplicated and by the book except for one strange detail: none of the Samaritans receive the Holy Spirit. Two of the apostles, Peter and John, have to make the trek from Jerusalem to pray for the Samaritans and lay their hands on them. Then the Spirit makes an entrance.

It's an odd scene, the coming of Peter and John, and it makes some readers nervous. It concerns those of us who disapprove of notions about spiritual authority organized or ranked according to hierarchies among human beings. Does the scene really ascribe special power to the apostles as dispensers of the Holy Spirit, putting the Spirit under their power or placing them above Philip? A wider survey of Acts suggests the answer is no, that the Spirit hardly resides under human beings' authority or needs a jump start through supercharged apostles. Sometimes the Spirit comes to people before they even express belief or are baptized (10:44–48). At other times the Spirit comes at baptism (19:5–6). The Holy Spirit in Acts never shows up according to a schedule but instead bursts onto the narrative stage, making a statement to those present. The variety among the Spirit's arrivals makes one thing clear: the Holy Spirit is free. Acts offers no simple formula to explain how the Spirit works. The Spirit will not be boxed in. People are subject to the Spirit; no one *possesses* the Spirit. Several other passages in Acts will reiterate this point when God leads the church into new understandings of its purpose and membership.

The question remains, however: what are Peter and John doing there, and what effects do their prayer and touch have? These apostles make the trip so *they* can learn something; they have not come to validate Philip's ministry or the Samaritans' conversion. They do not control who gets the Holy Spirit. In their prayer they acknowledge their and the Samaritans' dependence on God. In laying their hands on the new believers, they do not release the Spirit into them; rather, they declare their own solidarity with these new believers as God gives the Spirit. When the Spirit comes, *God* endorses Philip's ministry as part of Jesus's ongoing ministry through his followers. When the Spirit comes, God declares the unity between the Jerusalem church and this body of new, Samaritan believers. Peter and John come because God has them be assured for themselves, as representatives of the entire Jerusalem church, that these Samaritans are true members too. The scene allows God to tell Peter, John, and the rest of the community already in existence, "These Samarians are now your people, and you are theirs." It makes for a dramatic demonstration of inclusion and unity in the presence of all parties.

The new Christian community in Samaria receives very little attention in the overall story: just this scene and brief mentions of its ongoing existence later in Acts (9:31; 15:3). Nevertheless, in this passage we meet one Samaritan believer, a memorable one: a celebrity convert named Simon the Great.

Simon, we learn, practices magic, amazing the whole population "from the least to the greatest" with his powers. When the gospel comes to town, he believes it. He submits to baptism. Then he follows Philip around like a curious puppy, marveling at the miracles Philip performs.

When Simon observes the Holy Spirit's arrival as Peter and John place their hands on believers, his true colors emerge. Fervently he offers to purchase their power so he might impart the Spirit through his own hands. Peter responds with an acidic rebuke. Simon's attempt to purchase "God's gift" reveals his corrupt heart. Simon exposes himself as the antithesis of Philip and Peter, those through whom God works for the benefit of others. Simon clings to his reputation for "great"-ness, craving power in his new Christian identity. He hardly resembles others in Jerusalem who used their money to support their fellow believers (4:32–37).

As the scene comes to a close, the chastised Simon scarcely manifests the power of God or greatness of any kind. He must throw himself on God's mercy, even beseeching Peter and John's help. Acts remains silent about how his story ends in contrast to countless legends spun by later Christian authors in which he turns up as a persistent villain, an archetypical false believer and heretic.

Magicians appear occasionally in Acts (see 13:6 and 19:19), for the practice of magic was well known in the ancient world. Likewise,

Philip, Peter, Jesus, and others in Acts have company in performing miracles and healings. The basic belief was that wonder-workers, whether one labeled them as miracle workers or magicians, could tap into forces beyond ordinary human control. Therefore, Simon's "magic" would have looked more like Philip's miracles (healings and exorcisms) than the pulling-rabbits-out-of-hats illusions associated with "magicians" today.

While Acts identifies several followers of Jesus who perform miracles, others with special powers get labeled as magicians, and the narrative's attitude toward them is thoroughly negative. For one thing, an established Jewish perspective on magic associated it with the idolatrous practices of other nations and their false gods (Deuteronomy 18:9–14). Acts indicts magicians for using their craft selfishly, for financial gain (like Simon), or for retaining a grip on power (like another magician in 13:7–8). Acts understands magic as a lucrative practice rooted in a desire for power, and the narrative frequently presents economic greed as a sign of misplaced spiritual priorities. We witnessed this at close range in the story of Ananias and Sapphira (5:1–11), where greed, deceit, and manipulation functioned arm in arm. For another example, note the report of Judas Iscariot's death at the beginning of Acts, which underscores the profitable nature of treacherous deeds when it says Judas purchased a field with the money he was given to betray Jesus, a field finally polluted by his blood (1:18–19).

Simon the Great represents an attempt to exploit the gospel for one's own gain and glory. He eagerly desires the "power" (literally, "authority" in 8:19) to manipulate the Holy Spirit: more than undifferentiated power given by God—God's own presence! Simon's downfall tells a morality tale about the lure of power and the human desire to seize control over those things that usually resist our control, particularly other people and God's own self.

What makes Simon's lust for power especially worrisome is that it dwells in a man who apparently experiences an authentic conversion, having believed in the gospel and submitted to baptism. Instead of a dastardly infiltrator, he is, by all appearances, a newly minted insider. Perhaps he intends to use the power he desires for good and not for evil! But, even so, he illustrates the ways people can use even religious faith as a cover for exploiting and dominating others.

Our religious hypocrisy, when we embed it in religious institutions and language, can also shield us from God whenever we use it to close ourselves off from hearing God or from placing ourselves at God's mercy. Through the years Simon has had many imitators among those who find in Christianity a base of operations for pursuing their self-assertive ambitions and self-aggrandizing schemes.

Maybe this passage raises hopes that the gospel can expose these kinds of abuses and our propensity to hijack Christian faith and community to serve our own ends or glory. The intentions of God are to disarm evil, yet Acts repeatedly reminds us that deceit and opposition regularly beset the gospel's attempts to gain a foothold in our existence. At various stages in the gospel's advancement it encounters attempts to corrupt it through greed, exploitation, or evil. We saw this with Ananias and Sapphira (5:1–11); we see it here with Simon the Great; we will see it again with others who, when they encounter the gospel, manifest evil impulses through their unwillingness to part with their advantages and influence.

At the same time, others in Acts respond quite differently. They do not always receive as much attention as people like Simon, but they are there. Like the Samaritans who experience "great joy" in response to Philip's ministry. Like others who willingly set aside power and prestige to have a share in God's work on behalf of the world. These provide consistent, sometimes quiet, reminders of the gospel's true power as an expression of God's resolve to set things right. These reminders give hope that even a soul as twisted as Simon's might find forgiveness and a new beginning. The same hope therefore exists for my distracted soul, or for yours, or for that really annoying hypocrite I know, the one whose name I shouldn't put in a book.

After all, the power to make those kinds of transformations happen belongs ultimately to God, the only One we can trust with it.

Acts 8:26–40

Absurdly Good News

What is to prevent me from being baptized? (Acts 8:36)

This passage, in which Philip encounters a man who has been unfortunately remembered not by his name but inelegantly as "the Ethiopian eunuch," unfolds like a dream.

To call it a dream is to acknowledge the many details that lend it a fantastical quality. So much about it appears too good to be true, too fortuitous to be possible, too strange to be comfortable. But our dreams, as any armchair psychologist knows, are rarely pure fiction. They explain things. They help us imagine new possibilities when we think we have hit the limits of what we can perceive and should expect.

Philip's incredible adventure functions like that, challenging our limits. In Acts 8, now that the disciples' witness to Jesus has begun to venture outside Jerusalem, the narrative may make us think back to the promise that they, as Jesus said in 1:8, will reach "the ends of the earth," wherever that is.

The dream answers any questions about that with an unqualified yes. One way or another, by dumb luck or by design (Acts suggests the latter), the gospel will find ways to spread into new cultural landscapes. It will find a hearing. It really does have potential to disrupt the whole world, one interaction at a time.

The episode begins with one of God's messengers (the word *angel* means "messenger") instructing Philip to travel on a road extending from Jerusalem to the southwest, toward Gaza. As if receiving clear communication from an angel was not strange enough on its own, the specifics should attract attention. It is "a wilderness road," essentially a connector running through the middle of nowhere. Furthermore, the angel probably tells Philip to go there at midday. (As the NRSV's footnote indicates, the expression *go toward the south* in 8:26 can also mean "go at noon," which would make the angel's sentence less redundant.) A midday trek makes the story even wilder, as noon would not be an ideal time to encounter anyone traveling in a desertlike setting.

Philip nevertheless encounters someone, an extraordinary someone. He is African, a chief treasurer of a Nubian queen. Judging from her title, the Candace, she probably rules over Meroe, a well-established state south of Egypt. We may assume she enjoys considerable wealth, making this man quite influential and important in his society. (Possessing a scroll of the prophet Isaiah, he must have his own wealth and intercontinental connections.) His identity as a eunuch could have made him widely despised or mocked by the ancient readers of Acts, even as it also appears to accentuate his status as a trusted insider in the Candace's realm, for eunuchs could be counted on to fulfill certain duties with little risk of defiling royal bloodlines.

North of the Mediterranean Sea, ancient authors once spoke of Ethiopia as the outermost reach of the civilized world and Ethiopians as beautiful, impressive people. As "an Ethiopian," the eunuch conjures images of a person and culture exemplifying mystery and exoticism, in all the connotations of the word. If anyone in Acts represents, from the perspective of certain cultural stereotypes, the "other" or someone who dwells at the "edges," it is this figure. For most readers in a Roman-defined landscape, these associations would make this character a curiosity, a representative of people very different from themselves.

〜✍〜

The unexpected details continue. The man travels the road after a visit to Jerusalem to worship. He sits in his chariot reading the book of Isaiah. This complete foreigner studies and worships the God of Israel!

The precise nature of his worship remains unclear. There was at that time no uniform understanding of what it took to become a full proselyte to Judaism, and parts of the Jerusalem temple were segregated, limiting some worship options exclusively to full-fledged Jewish males. Gentiles were permitted in a large segment of the temple compound, and we should probably understand the Ethiopian as a gentile who is attracted to Judaism. As a eunuch, he may bring to mind some parts of the law of Moses prohibiting castrated men from full participation in the worshiping assembly (Deuteronomy 23:1; Leviticus 21:16–23). But nothing in Acts 8 calls attention to this man's having been denied the chance to participate in worship according to how he wanted. That is, he does not depart Jerusalem resentful of his experience there.

At the same time, he does leave Jerusalem with questions. When Philip approaches the chariot he hears the man reading aloud (which was normal practice during this era) from Isaiah 53:7–8. When the Ethiopian asks Philip about the passage, he asks a question Old Testament scholars continue to debate today: who exactly is Isaiah talking about? We do not hear Philip's response, but we must assume he takes the words describing an innocent sufferer as an opportunity to speak about Jesus's death and resurrection. It is difficult to imagine another question that would set the table so well for a presentation about the gospel of Jesus Christ.

The eunuch's hospitality and openness permeate his brief interaction with Philip. This strikes a noticeable contrast with Simon the magician earlier in Acts 8, whose exposure to the gospel resulted in a desire to exploit spiritual power for his own advantage.

The next wonder in this idealistic scene occurs when the chariot comes across a pool of water alongside the wilderness road. This perfectly orchestrated meeting keeps getting better. Indicating his enthusiasm for Philip's message, the Ethiopian asks an interesting question: "What is to prevent me from being baptized?"

What would "prevent" him? Perhaps his phrasing of the question asserts a conviction: he knows the answer is nothing, for nothing about the gospel involves restrictions against certain kinds of outsiders. Maybe another part of Isaiah comes into view for him here, namely, the assurances about eunuchs and foreigners coming to belong to God's people.

> Do not let the foreigner joined to the LORD say,
>   "The LORD will surely separate me from his people";
> and do not let the eunuch say,
>   "I am just a dry tree."
> For thus says the LORD:
> To the eunuchs who keep my sabbaths,
>   who choose the things that please me
>   and hold fast my covenant,
> I will give, in my house and within my walls,
>   a monument and a name
>   better than sons and daughters;
> I will give them an everlasting name
>   that shall not be cut off.
>
> And the foreigners who join themselves to the LORD,
>   to minister to him, to love the name of the LORD,
>   and to be his servants,
> all who keep the sabbath, and do not profane it,
>   and hold fast my covenant—
> these I will bring to my holy mountain,
>   and make them joyful in my house of prayer;
> their burnt offerings and their sacrifices
>   will be accepted on my altar;
> for my house shall be called a house of prayer
>   for all peoples.
> Thus says the Lord GOD,
>   who gathers the outcasts of Israel,
> I will gather others to them
>   besides those already gathered. (Isaiah 56:3–8)

Does the Ethiopian recognize that familiar promises about God's universal, inclusive reach are now coming to fruition, at least for him? If so, his theological hunches paint him as less an outsider than some might have assumed. He and Philip interpret Scripture together in light of the gospel.

The Ethiopian's question, "What is to prevent me from being baptized?" may also reiterate the utter improbability of the scene. Apparently God has coordinated all sorts of unlikely coincidences so far, and so the appearance of water in the desert makes the queen's official gleefully cry out, essentially, "Well, would you look at that! Now we stumble upon a desert oasis! Resistance to all that's happening here is futile!"

Acts gives readers little time to digest the whole scene, as the Spirit of the Lord immediately removes Philip, setting him on a path to minister elsewhere, while the eunuch returns home in great joy, perhaps to propagate the gospel in his homeland. (Christian authors in the subsequent centuries celebrate this man as an evangelist and the founder of Christian churches in Ethiopia and Sudan.)

This strange and amusing story tells us very little in explicit terms about God and the nature of God's business on behalf of humanity, although it offers intimations about Jesus's resemblance to the humiliated sufferer of Isaiah 53. The only dialogue we overhear is questions the two men put to one another. We must read between the lines to discover answers.

The answers come in what the passage shows. It's a story about exquisite, though incredible, matchmaking.

The matchmaking, which God orchestrates through the angel's instructions to Philip, aims to instill confidence in God. God exhibits a flair for the dramatic in ensuring the work of Jesus's witnesses, even though persecution has disrupted their lives and broken up the harmonious existence of their community in Jerusalem.

The matchmaking also says something about the world waiting "out there" for the word of God to come to it. The presentation of the eunuch relies on ancient stereotypes polluted by xenophobia, certainly. Within that setting and with a kind of romantic, compelling strangeness, the eunuch represents new audiences waiting to hear about the gospel. The passage stokes confidence about venues the gospel has yet to find. Even the places that the book's original readers might consider new, unfamiliar, distant, or curious await the gospel. It can fit even there.

At the same time, this "other" comes across as no naif or stranger in need of socialization *into* an established Christian worldview. He contributes to the abbreviated theological conversation; he's partly responsible for expanding the emerging sense of what the gospel means for people. No apostle has to venture to Africa to lay hands on him. He journeys on, bearing the gospel himself, just as Philip and others do in the places they travel.

Sometimes in Acts the word of God finds audiences through amazing ways (as in this scene); in other passages it happens through unimpressive or matter-of-fact circumstances (as when Paul goes to Athens in Acts 17). When God brings the Ethiopian and Philip together so ideally, with such an orderly fit, we should not assume we have found a model for what successful outreach must look like. There is no promise here that God will make the gospel's expansion an easy thing or that this event is normal.

If we make the orderly matchmaking the central feature of this passage, we encounter problems. In the book's desire to underscore God's commitment to ensuring the spread and vitality of the gospel, Acts might lead us to wonder whether coincidences really exist, or whether every set of circumstances must point to some kind of divine purpose. If we lose sight of this story's fantastical tone, we might slide down a slippery slope toward assuming that God will determine which team will win the next World Series or that the dead car battery preventing me from getting to an appointment is God's way of teaching me to be more patient. I suspect God is more interested in a person's ability to react to any and all situations with grace and faith than in a person trying to imagine how God might have manufactured a set of circumstances to make a point. Otherwise, we're only one tsunami or tornado away from a theological conundrum that might paint God as a monster. Circumstances, whether tragic or beneficial, are usually just that: circumstances.

Any dream can distort reality if we confuse it with reality instead of allowing it to inform how we perceive and approach reality.

Dreams require interpretation. As the Ethiopian eunuch realizes, interpretation happens best through conversation with others. Our interpretation of this story needs to enjoy its weirdness by naming it as weird, even as we can playfully dig into the story's idealism to ask what it says about God and God's commitment to humanity—all of humanity.

This passage dreams less about God's control over everything and more about God's unwavering commitment to working through all people for the sake of all people. It's as if God knows too well how small and confined our imaginations can become, because we think we can figure everything out through our cold calculations about what's possible and what's feasible.

Dreams shouldn't allow dreamers to nourish fantasies that they're the center of the universe. At their best, dreams remind us to expect surprises, to open ourselves up, and never to be too sure about where and how something will finally end.

Acts 9:1–30

Seeing a Different Reality

> And immediately something like scales fell from his eyes,
> and his sight was restored. (Acts 9:18)

The account of Saul's encounter with the risen Jesus Christ might be the best known of all the stories Acts tells. In fact, Acts may offer it to readers as the most important story in the whole book, since it appears three times: here, then retold twice by Paul (the name Acts uses for Saul from 13:9 onward) to different audiences in Acts 22 and 26.

Interestingly, the three accounts do not completely agree among themselves. It is not so unusual, we know, to embellish or emphasize certain details in a story, depending on what a storyteller thinks an audience should hear in a given setting. Both times Paul recounts the event later in Acts, he strains to establish his credibility in the eyes of an angry mob and high-ranking Roman officials, respectively. Clearly, what happens to Saul during his journey to Damascus stands at the center of his understanding of who God is and what God expects from him.

Readers have already met Saul before he steps into the narrator's spotlight in 9:1. He briefly occupied a place of prominence in 7:58, when a furious crowd killed Stephen, the first of Jesus's followers to die at the hands of opponents in Acts. Some of those opponents lay their outer cloaks at Saul's feet, a curious and unexplained detail. Does it single out Saul as the lynching's ringleader, or is it more innocent, merely indicating the man who happened to be standing near the clothing pile? In either case, Saul thought Stephen got what he deserved, according to 8:1.

It doesn't matter whether Acts first introduced Saul as someone already opposed to the gospel who therefore sanctioned Stephen's death or whether the grisly incident he witnessed somehow compelled him to take up persecution as his own avocation. Almost immediately after Stephen expired, Acts highlights Saul as a key figure in "a severe persecution," a man busy "ravaging the church" by incarcerating its men and women (8:1–3). Acts does not explain Saul's motives or even what might authorize him to prosecute people in this way; he appears merely as a Jew determined to halt the spread of the gospel and to intimidate his fellow Jews—males and females—who identify as Jesus's followers.

Therefore, Acts 9 begins with a sense of, "Meanwhile, back to Saul and his contributions to the severe persecution mentioned a while ago. . . ." It is not enough for Saul to drive Jesus's disciples out of Jerusalem; he intends to track them down and parade them back to the big city in chains. He heads for Damascus, a city in Syria over a hundred miles to the northeast of Jerusalem. He will indeed return to Jerusalem by the end of the chapter, but not as the same person.

On the road to Damascus, a blinding light and a disembodied voice cause Saul to find himself in the dust. (Medieval art shows him falling off a horse, but Acts says nothing about animals being present.) The voice belongs to Jesus, who says Saul persecutes *him*. Saul may have thought he was persecuting the church, but in doing so he persecutes Jesus himself. This reiterates the description of the church back in Acts 4–5, which identified God so closely with the life of the Christian community that Ananias and Sapphira's deceit against that community equaled deceit against God.

It can be tempting to understand what happens to Saul (falling to the ground, experiencing blindness, having to be led by the hand) as humiliation meant to punish him for the violence he has perpetrated to this point. But a better interpretation is to see it as an enactment of the gospel. Saul embodies reversal; or, reversal happens to him when Jesus disrupts his expectation.

Saul changes from seeing to being blind. His confident persecutor's zeal gives way to confessed ignorance about the "Lord" he cannot recognize on his own.

He changes from a man intending to lead captives to Jerusalem in chains to one forced to be led into Damascus by others. His authority over others' bodies transforms into his own dependence.

He changes from a man on a mission to one who must wait to learn what to do next. Previously he actively petitioned the high priest in Jerusalem to endorse his plans, but now he fasts in anticipation of receiving further instructions.

He changes from a man exercising great power over the church to one overpowered by Jesus.

In what ways can such reversals enact the gospel? Frequently Luke and Acts look to dynamic disruptions as indications of God at work. When God's intentions are realized, the normal states of affairs are turned upside down. The praise spoken by Mary, Jesus's mother, in the Gospel of Luke provides the most poignant example when she says, describing God,

> He has shown strength with his arm;
>   he has scattered the proud in the thoughts of their hearts.
> He has brought down the powerful from their thrones,
>   and lifted up the lowly;
> he has filled the hungry with good things,
>   and sent the rich away empty. (Luke 1:51–53)

Mary offered a character sketch of God, saying these kinds of reversals are God's typical behavior, expressing God's intentions for a just society. As a poor, insignificant, unmarried virgin confidently expecting to give birth to a mighty, God-appointed ruler, Mary praised God for confounding usual expectations about what real power looks like. Promises about the strong being humiliated and the lowly being exalted proclaim God as the world's ultimate authority, even as they

depict the justice dear to God's heart. A God capable of feeding the
hungry and overturning kingdoms cannot be constrained by "the
way things are."

Reversal does not need to be a zero-sum game, in which every
winner is offset by a loser, or the lowly get their turn at oppressing
the mighty. The divine upheavals Mary celebrated could sound like
bad news to Saul as he fasts in Damascus, but the narrative won't
fully support this assumption. Nothing suggests his suffering comes
to him as payback or for its own sake, as if suffering will "fix" him
or even the score. Instead, Saul's sudden reversal reminds all who will
encounter him, throughout the pages of Acts, that he operates as a
witness to God's work. Any qualities of Saul's that might make him
appear impressive to his contemporaries melt away in his encounter with Jesus. Any successes or accomplishments from this point
forward happen not because of his talents or status but because of
God's choice to manifest the gospel through Saul's life and words.

Saul's reversal will also redound to others to benefit them as re-
cipients of God's salvation. As he puts it in a later retelling of this
conversation with Jesus, his reversal will result in him going now to
gentiles "to open their eyes so that they may turn from darkness to
light and from the power of Satan to God" (26:18). Others need
to know the truth Saul is coming to comprehend in Damascus as
his own eyes are reopened. Others need their situations reversed,
their ignorance and oppression upended. The focus stays on Saul's
significance for others, and it remains there as this passage continues
into its second half.

God's activity in Acts often involves God working different sides of
a story at the same time. Recall Philip being so easily set up to explain
a passage from Isaiah to the eunuch returning to Ethiopia. In Acts 10,
God will work separately through both Peter and a Roman centurion
for people to recognize God's intention to accomplish something new.
A similar thing happens after Saul's initial shock, when we meet a
new character named Ananias.

Saul harassed "disciples" (9:1); in Damascus, someone identified
simply as a "disciple" helps him complete his transformation from

persecutor to proclaimer. Just as Jesus initiates contact with Saul and calls him to a new understanding, Ananias of Damascus receives an unexpected vision of Jesus. This experience brings Ananias, who needs a little convincing, to see Saul in a totally new light. Ananias can be forgiven for his initial resistance when he tries to tell Jesus just how dangerous a person this Saul is. In the conversation, Jesus redefines Saul for Ananias: Saul's past and reputation no longer adequately express who he is; now Jesus has chosen him as his own "instrument" to convey the gospel to "Gentiles and kings and . . . the people of Israel."

Ananias plays an obviously crucial role in authenticating Saul's transformed identity. Why would anyone trust the new Saul? What would prevent Saul and his traveling companions from gradually doubting the genuineness of their memories of the voice on the road? An additional witness to Saul's life-altering encounter helps everyone. When God dramatically reorients expectations and causes people to reassess what's possible, everyone needs to be converted. Our old ways of seeing people, situations, and even the gospel are too ingrained in our minds to go away easily. Through Ananias, God provides one more strong nudge for everyone to see things differently.

Furthermore, Jesus has plans for Saul, plans extending beyond this scene alone. Jesus tells Ananias about Saul's future: Saul will bear witness to Jesus among people who have not yet heard the gospel message in Acts: gentiles and Roman governors. Saul will do so not as an individual, charismatic outlier but as a member of the community of disciples. We see this when the passage concludes and its reversals come full circle, when Saul returns to Jerusalem and attempts to join with the believers who remain there. Barnabas has to take and lead Saul into this community because the others continue to see him as his former self and mistrust him. In responding to Jesus, Saul does not embark on a career as a lone follower. He must become part of something, the church that God is forming. In doing so, he immediately affirms what Jesus told Ananias: Saul will bear Jesus's name to others, and he will endure great hardship as part of his efforts.

Acts does not flinch when it speaks of people seeing visions and hearing Jesus speak. Even so, such religious experiences were hardly commonplace in the ancient world; nor were people back then credulous enough to trust every report of a vision. Still, passages like this one leave many of us disoriented by their foreign character. The danger lies in allowing our questions about extraordinary phenomena to distract us into assuming that the visions are the most important pieces of the story or that they are the typical or required way of discerning God's point of view. What's important here is not that Saul sees a flash and hears a voice, nor that Ananias encounters Jesus. Rather, the key detail is that each of the men's experiences lends the story an expanded vision of what's real and what's possible. Each of them credits those new perspectives to Jesus's activity in their midst.

New perspectives rarely take hold easily. They often require something outside of ourselves—an idea, a message, another person—to confront us with new evidence or new possibilities. Actively embracing new hopes of what might be possible for us or for our world can take our faith on a white-knuckle ride. Ananias knows the feeling; at first he answers back to correct Jesus, but eventually he comes around and walks into a house where the church's presumed archenemy waits for him.

Something makes Ananias willing to trust that something besides threats and murder can be possible for Saul. Ananias's vision probably does not give him confidence all by itself. The impulse has to come from deeper places too, from the foundations of his understanding of who God is. It may also derive from his openness to the wild reversals God can accomplish, whether those involve elevating someone vulnerable like Mary or reconfiguring a powerful person like Saul.

I've never heard God speak out loud, nor do I expect to. But I know trustworthy people who swear they have. I also know and have read about many people who found themselves in positions where their gifts auspiciously aligned with others' needs. These are people who—whether it was through creativity, crisis, luck, or providence—suddenly found themselves able to help. Or they found themselves compelled to discover a way to provide help because they sensed the good news of God's salvation could be expressed somehow through their assistance, love, teaching, or simple availability.

Maybe that's what it sounds and looks like when God summons a person to do something. Sometimes new connections and a re-directed perspective just happen. Sometimes people risk, or just show up. Maybe discovery and engaged resolve to work toward different realities sometimes indicate that people have encountered and heard from God, whether they describe it that way or not.

Acts conditions its readers to be ready for God to grant visions, whether those come in extraordinary sights and sounds or they present themselves—as I have experienced—through the insights of visionary and attentive people. The church that Acts imagines, if we recall the descriptions of the Jerusalem community at the end of both Acts 2 and 4, is one that through its very cooperative existence creates a state of affairs that defies humanity's common tendencies toward distrust and isolation. We dismiss the possibility of gaining new or renewed vision when we draw our established perceptions with indelible lines. What if God continues to surprise and disrupt us as we adopt new outlooks on what's possible, just as God surprises Saul and Ananias with promises of a different identity and an enlarged future?

Acts 9:32–43

The Work, Pain, and Tenderness of Christian Service

Tabitha, get up. (Acts 9:40)

The Bible's miracle stories elicit various reactions from us. Because they evoke wonder, they occupy prominent places in children's Sunday school curricula and children's Bibles. They can encourage people who have lost hope or who cling to fading faith in God's ability to illuminate a way out of suffering and powerlessness. They make others skeptical, wondering how much the stories stem from legends, superstitions, or ancient ignorance about how the world really works. Sometimes, honestly, they worry us, making us wonder if the comparatively bland Christianity we practice today bears enough resemblance to what the Christian life might have been like back in the day, when apostles healed the sick and raised the dead.

Because Jesus performs so many miracles in the Gospels, it doesn't take much analysis to recognize that his contemporaries regarded him as a wonder-worker. Notice that none of his opponents in the Gospels ever accuses him of being a charlatan who fakes miracles to get attention. They recognize some kind of power at work in him and question its true source. Does he work as one authorized by God, or is he satanic (see Luke 11:15–20 and 20:1–2)? We cannot dissect what people experienced when Jesus performed these kinds of acts, and Christian faith does not depend on our ability to either accept or explain away every instance of the Gospels' descriptions of his doing something that seems to defy our understanding of medicine or physics.

But things are a little different in Acts, where Jesus's followers are the ones performing miracles. This implies that Jesus imparts power to them. (He did so to the apostles in Luke 9:1–2. And, in Luke 24:49 and Acts 1:8, he described the Holy Spirit as a source of "power.") If he imparted power to them, where is that power today? I know many suffering people who would like to benefit from it. And I have a hunch that attendance at my church could increase dramatically if our leaders started healing the sick and raising the dead every Sunday morning on schedule at 10:30 a.m.

When Peter heals a paralyzed man and raises a woman from the dead in Lydda and Joppa, two cities northwest of Jerusalem (roughly 25 and 35 miles away, respectively), these are not his first efforts in the miracle-working department (see, for example, 5:12–16). But it is significant that Acts takes time to tell these two stories, bidding us to pay closer attention.

For one thing, the narrative treats those who are healed as more than objects; we learn their names. He doesn't heal "a paralyzed man"; he heals Aeneas. The dead woman in Joppa is named Tabitha, and she is greatly revered by those close to her. Others call her Dorcas, because she has two names, one Aramaic and one Greek (each word means "gazelle" in its own language). Perhaps she herself is multicultural, able to circulate among a variety of ethnic contexts, connecting people across their differences just like the gospel in which she has a share.

Aeneas has known suffering. For eight years he remained bedridden. We learn much more about Tabitha, and Aeneas's story quickly gets relegated as mostly a precursor to hers. She is a "disciple," a believer, one of the clan. But her discipleship is exemplary; in her generosity, she is a leader within her community. Perhaps this explains why Peter was summoned to Joppa: because the believers there considered her necessary to their corporate well-being.

Tabitha's general reputation, we learn right away, involves good works and acts of charity. She is a giver, someone who puts her own resources toward meeting others' needs. When this fast-paced, action-oriented book slows for a few verses, we receive a tender look into the particular details of what makes this disciple so great. Among other deeds, she made clothing for widows. Her work was creative; she turned cloth into clothing to provide garments for people who we can presume were poor. No wonder these widows, women already acquainted with loss and grief, weep at her death. Their tears express deep love for her and perhaps concern for their own future. The details sprinkled throughout these verses force us to linger over what a loss Tabitha's death represents.

Members of her community wash her corpse, according to custom. A group summons Peter to Joppa. It seems they want him to do something to comfort or help them and their wider community. Or maybe they dare to hope he might do something for *her*. But can this wonder-working apostle do something so impossible? Can he raise the dead and thus restore life to a whole community in need?

He can, and he does. In a scene very reminiscent of Luke 8:40–42, 49–56, where Jesus brings a young girl back from death, Peter raises Tabitha.

Or, more accurately, Jesus raises Tabitha. Acts carefully avoids giving the impression that Peter possesses this power on his own. He prays before commanding Tabitha to rise. When Jesus revivified Jairus's daughter, he did not pray but only addressed the girl directly (Luke 8:54). Likewise, recall the earlier verses in this passage, when Peter says to Aeneas, "Jesus Christ heals you; get up and make your bed!" Peter does not replace Jesus; he acts as a channel through whom Jesus's ministry continues.

These miracles direct us toward a pattern in Acts that we've already glimpsed in part. The main characters engage in ministries that closely resemble Jesus's ministry. The portraits of Peter and Paul, in particular, recall the depiction of Jesus in Luke's Gospel. All three preach frequently and face consistent opposition, and more specific deeds draw additional parallels.

Event	Jesus	Peter	Paul
A paralyzed person is healed.	Luke 5:17–26	Acts 3:1–10; 9:32–35	Acts 14:8–11
People are healed by touching a healer or things extending from him (clothing, shadows, handkerchiefs).	Luke 6:17–19; 8:43–46	Acts 5:12–16	Acts 19:11–12
A dead person is brought back to life.	Luke 7:11–17; 8:40–56	Acts 9:36–43	Acts 20:7–12
Satanic deterrents are opposed and defeated.	Luke 4:1–13; Acts 10:36–38	Acts 5:1–6	Acts 13:4–11
Opponents arrest and detain the healers.	Luke 22:47–65	Acts 4:1–4; 5:17–18; 12:1–5	Acts 16:19–24; 21:30–22:24

The parallels contribute to more than literary artistry. They reiterate something about Jesus's relationship to his followers. Peter and Paul, as well as others in Acts, mirror Jesus's activity as evidence that they continue Jesus's ministry. The work of the church in Acts is not a new thing; it is a continuation. Jesus continues to be active in the world through the deeds of his followers—through miracles, through the messages proclaimed, through accomplishing God's salvation.

Jesus remains present, then, through the church. Yet Acts refuses to imply that the church or its prominent members *replace* Jesus or stand on par with him. Peter and Paul may suffer hardship, be arrested, and find themselves on trial before authorities. But we never read in Acts about their deaths. By keeping those events off the narrative stage, Acts discourages us from attaching too much importance to Peter and Paul. Others can do the things they do; they are not irreplaceable. Only Jesus dies, rises again, ascends, and sends the Spirit. As Peter himself says in 4:12, "There is salvation in no one else, for there is no other name under heaven given among mortals by which we must be saved."

Acts also pulls attention from Peter and his prominence when it refrains from making much of Peter's fame as a result of these miracles. Aeneas's and Tabitha's restorations garner attention: with a strong measure of hyperbole, the text reports that "all the residents of Lydda and Sharon" saw Aeneas back on his feet, and news of Tabitha's return from death spreads "throughout Joppa." As a result, no one "follows Peter" or "joins the church"; instead, many put their faith in, or turn to, "the Lord." The power working in Peter derives from Jesus, and it reverts back to Jesus in that it brings others into his fold. While compassion surely motivates these miracles, it seems their ultimate aim involves attracting others to the good news.

The miracles Peter performs are not, therefore, ends in themselves. They provide a means of bearing witness to Jesus as new expressions of the ministry he began after his baptism. This ministry accomplishes many things for those it affects: Aeneas certainly benefits in terms of health and finances when his paralysis goes away, and the widows of Joppa must rejoice in the return of their friend and benefactor. Because she lives, they become less vulnerable. Tabitha is probably pleased too. But, at the same time, these values are temporary. We assume Aeneas will eventually grow old and frail, and Tabitha will one day die—again—as will the widows and other disciples who need her. Peter, even as a conduit of Jesus's power, cannot fix all the world's woes. The miracles do not pretend to suggest he can.

Acts includes its share of high-profile figures, people like Peter and Paul, who sometimes tempt us to believe that authentic discipleship must be a high-wire act, always involving threat and deliverance, public recognition and miraculous deeds. These characters easily distract us, and even unsettle us, if we presume that their experiences are normative, what's expected of all disciples at all times and places.

But then Tabitha steps into the spotlight.

Here is a disciple who proves just as exemplary, just as necessary to the well-being of her community. The beauty about Tabitha and her briefly described service resides in how attainable her disciple-ship appears to us. Good works, charity, clothing the needy—hardly superhuman deeds, and yet still these activities can have nearly mi-raculous outcomes when they generate widespread love, support, and appreciation. She is every bit as much a disciple and a witness as Peter. In her commitment to others, she leads her community. In her mercy, we see God.

At the same time, a risk remains in sentimentalizing Tabitha or imagining that Acts recognizes no difference between her and Peter.

Acts devotes a mere seven verses to Tabitha, quite a few more to the apostle. Peter and Paul, and the public deeds they perform, provide the book's structure. Quieter disciples, along with all of the named and unnamed female characters in Acts, get relegated to supporting, more hidden roles. The author of Acts may or may not have intended to reinforce such a stark separation between different kinds of discipleship or different kinds of disciples, but the separation impresses itself upon many readers. It is, for me, one of the most frustrating things about Acts and how the book has been used over the centuries to endorse particular kinds of ministry as most valuable and to limit women's and others' access to certain ministerial responsibilities. Other New Testament writings, such as Romans 16:1–16, preserve a different record of women's participation in early churches' public leadership. Acts could have told us more.

There's something worth emphasizing, then, in Tabitha's seven little verses. We can still see her and extol her value. The narrative opens the window into her life just far enough for us to peer inside and appreciate how vital she is to those around her. We duly celebrate her for her service to others, for the ways she manifests God's own concern and charity.

We also learn from her two names, which invite us to imagine the bridges she might build between different kinds of people. Although such cultural bridges may appear insignificant at this point in the story, they will not when the very next chapter of Acts has concluded, once Peter discovers a new dimension of the gospel's universal reach.

Maybe the woman some called Tabitha and others called Dorcas knew all along the important things Peter has yet to learn.

Acts 10:1–11:18

Old Boundaries Obliterated

> Then God has given even to the Gentiles the repentance
> that leads to life. (Acts 11:18)

Sometimes it takes an act of God to convince us that deeply established assumptions about God and our world suddenly have to change.

Jesus was a Jew. His closest followers were all Jews. The Christian community that settled and grew in Jerusalem before persecution scattered it at the beginning of Acts 8—all of its members were Jewish or had previously converted to Judaism. In Acts 1–9 we saw a movement growing and expressing itself within Judaism, incorporating the Jews' long-lost, long-alienated relatives from Samaria as well, and no one—except for a certain Ethiopian eunuch—appears to expect it will be any other way. Words spoken by Jesus and others about his significance for "the gentiles," "all the families of the earth," and "all nations" (Luke 2:32; 24:47; Acts 3:25; 9:15) have not captured anyone's imagination until we reach Acts 10:1–11:18. At this point, God initiates a whole new direction in the life of the church: God declares that old distinctions between Jews and gentiles can no longer hold as they once did, and God gives the Holy Spirit to gentiles. Despite the tremendous significance of this initiation, still it comes on a rather localized scale and is recognized only gradually by those who participate in the key events. For fuller recognition to occur, the people involved will need to hang on for the ride a while longer.

The story of Peter meeting Cornelius is a long one, as scenes in Acts go, and it offers much for readers to consider about changes in the composition of the early church. Certainly the most dramatic, formational, and unexpected thing that happened during the first three decades of the Christian church's history was the movement's transition from communities comprising Jews and proselytes to Judaism into communities that included gentiles on equal terms and with no preconditions as fellow members and co-beneficiaries of God's grace. The transition was not merely demographic but also theological, for it compelled Jesus's followers to explain how it could be that not requiring gentile converts to follow Jewish law (the law of Moses) rightly expressed God's intentions. Deeply ingrained customs were on the line: circumcision, dietary laws, Sabbath observance, and other practices formed important pieces of what it meant to identify as Jews and to submit one's whole self to God in response to divine mercy.

The means by which Acts tells, retells, then retells again the stories of Peter's and Cornelius's experiences demonstrate a literary artistry that underscores this passage's importance for the book's understanding of God's activity through, around, and out ahead of the church. In keeping with our focus on God and how Acts shapes our understanding of God's connection to our lives, our exploration of this account must leave some of its details unaddressed so we can focus on the larger picture.

From the way the passage begins we recognize it as another story in which God is quite involved. God initiates a series of events when both of the primary human characters—Cornelius and Peter—receive messages. The centurion speaks with an angel; the apostle sees a vision and hears the voice of the Lord. Still, these unusual events do not reveal what will happen next or what it all means. Peter, Cornelius, and others do not come to their insights until they gather together once everything concludes. If we skip ahead to 11:18 and read the passage's final verse, we learn the consensus that will be reached when Peter's associates in Jerusalem consider his report and all that has transpired and declare, "Then God has given even to the Gentiles the repentance that leads to life." Not "The church has changed" or "This new direction seems like a good idea to try," but "*God* has done something. *God* has brought life to the gentiles, through the gospel." (In Acts 5:31, Peter and others spoke of God giving "repentance" to the people of Israel through Jesus. Remember from the exploration of Acts 2–4: this repentance includes more than changed behavior; it refers primarily to arriving at a new understanding of God and the salvation God has made possible through Jesus Christ.)

The statement in 11:18 about what God has done for gentiles holds true not only for Cornelius and his relatives and friends; the believers in Jerusalem who utter it take Cornelius's experience as a dramatic in-breaking of a new, grand reality. In giving the Holy Spirit to gentiles, God takes the church down a road it did not expect to travel. Everyone involved in the story experiences surprise: Cornelius, Peter, their immediate associates, and those who hear Peter tell his story back in Jerusalem. All of them are converted in these verses as they come to understand something they did not foresee about the scope of the gospel and the growth of the church. God points them all in a new direction, and off they go. Although other figures, such as Simeon in Luke 2:29–32, grasped in a general sense what the coming of Jesus would mean for gentiles, Peter moves ahead in this passage apparently without the benefit of any authoritative teaching or clear precedent from Jesus.

Back at the passage's beginning, Cornelius enters the story accompanied by the narrator's affirmation of his exemplary piety. Although this man has a strong attraction to the God of Israel, this hardly erases his and his companions' status as gentiles. Indeed, the narrative takes steps to underscore both his religious ignorance and the separation between him and Peter as gentile and Jew. For one thing, humorously suggesting a propensity for polytheistic gentiles to worship anything, Cornelius falls at Peter's feet when the apostle enters his home. Also, Peter calls it "unlawful" for him to enter Cornelius's house, although "unseemly" is more technically accurate. Merely by offering hospitality to Cornelius's messengers in Joppa and then entering the centurion's home in Caesarea, Peter crosses deeply demarcated cultural lines meant to distinguish and protect God's holiness and Jews' distinctive identity as God's people. Later, in Acts 11, when Peter faces questions from other Jewish believers, the basis of their complaint is not that he preached the gospel to gentiles; it's that he got too close to people who were thought to deserve the label "profane" or "unclean." A major point of the story, the one that Peter and his Jerusalem colleagues learn through God's prompting, is that these kinds of labels are God's to determine and to remove, not humanity's.

The irony, of course, is that the people in Jerusalem in Acts 11 worry that Peter has denigrated God's holiness by getting too close to Cornelius when in fact he has merely obeyed God's leading. Once he hears Cornelius tell about his vision, the pieces fall into place for Peter. He finally declares, "I truly understand that God shows no partiality." God's impartiality means something other than disinterestedness; it expresses God's active concern for *all* humanity and God's desire to welcome all peoples. This would not have been a brand new theological insight for Peter and his Jewish contemporaries (assuming they know the Jewish scriptures), but the scene emphasizes the shocking manner in which God declares it, apparently overriding long-standing standards previously put in place to manage interactions between Jews and gentiles. A tectonic shift starts to occur in understanding and expressing what it means to be God's people.

What gets Peter to comprehend God as the One who shows "no partiality"? His vision helps, as does the hospitality both men extend in response to what God tells them to do. So too do Peter's memories of Jesus; when he tells Cornelius about him, he highlights evidence of God's impartiality. He says that Jesus is Lord of *all* (10:36). Because God was with him, Jesus healed *all* who were oppressed (10:38). Release from sins now comes to *everyone* who believes in him (10:43). At the same time, the source of this salvation for all remains very particular, rooted in God's actions through Jesus Christ, who was sent specifically "to the people of Israel" (10:36) and who proclaimed his message in Galilee and Judea (10:37, 39). Subsequent encounters with the risen Christ were also circumscribed, limited to Jesus's followers in the days after the resurrection (10:40–41). This particularity does not, however, limit the effects. Jesus reaffirmed God's faithfulness to the people of Israel; therefore, all the peoples of the world can trust God as the source of their salvation.

Throughout the sermon, Peter identifies God as the agent behind all aspects of the life, ministry, death, and resurrection of Jesus. This is not an especially surprising claim in light of the other sermons in Acts. But the rhetoric fits the setting, and it further affirms that God is broadening the horizons: because *God* was active through Jesus, Jesus's story attests *God* as welcoming of all. Remembering Jesus's story, Peter confirms what he may have suspected his vision of a sheet full of unclean animals was all about in the first place. If Peter were to borrow words from Simeon in Luke 2:29–32, he might say now that God, through Jesus Christ, has prepared salvation "in the presence of all peoples." Peter spots direct connections between the surprising work of God in his and Cornelius's experiences (the visions and the mutual hospitality), on one hand, and the salvation he has come to know (expressed in the life, death, and resurrection of Jesus Christ), on the other. What Peter sees at work between him and Cornelius is an outgrowth of what Jesus demonstrates about God's far-reaching intentions, hardly a deviation from it.

The coming of the Holy Spirit dramatically confirms all of this, even as it interrupts Peter's sermon. Peter and his Jewish colleagues interpret the Spirit's arrival as decisive, for they recognize the gentiles' experience as equal to their own (10:47; 11:15). Whether Jew or gentile, each receives from God the same gift, a gift of God's own presence. Therefore God has fulfilled a promise extended to each (recall 2:39). Were Peter to question these gentiles' new status or to reassert old dividing lines, it would be nothing less than impeding God (11:17). By bestowing the same Spirit upon both Jews and gentiles, God creates not just a relationship between the two groups but a unity. When with his friends in Jerusalem he looks back on the experience, Peter doesn't diminish the newness of what has transpired, but he does note its consistency with something Jesus said previously: "John baptized with water, but you will be baptized with the Holy Spirit" (11:16; see 1:5). God might be opening up new realities, but they are realities consistent with everything Jesus said and did.

In the earliest chapters of Acts, Peter's public sermons repeatedly called his Jewish audiences to recognize and embrace Jesus as God's means of bringing the salvation promised long ago to the people of Israel. In the story of Peter and Cornelius, more recognition and embracing happens, but this time Peter does it. Naming God's activity and perceiving the consequences of the gospel are not easy. Peter needs time. He needs to consult with others. He needs to hear Cornelius tell about his experiences. He needs to revisit things Jesus said. He needs the story to play itself out for a little bit. In the midst of all the visions, travel, and conversations, it looks impossible to know for sure what all the excitement means. Everything makes more sense once the story is done. That's usually the way it is when we speak about recognizing God. Those kinds of recognitions are rarely self-evident. Discerning God's intentions and altering our assumptions about people and how to live are always acts of faith. They involve daring to imagine new or unexpected possibilities; sometimes such possibilities correspond with old traditions, and sometimes they reshape them.

This passage about Peter and Cornelius does not dwell on the practical consequences of the development it describes: God giving "even to the Gentiles the repentance that leads to life." But it does offer hints about what will follow from this repentance. For example, much of the story describes instances of hospitality, people welcoming others into their homes. In fact, Peter's receipt of gentile hospitality seems to his friends in Jerusalem the most offensive aspect of what happens. When the people involved in this story recognize God's activity in freely welcoming gentiles, their hospitable interactions with one another take on greater significance. In welcoming gentiles into the family of God, God does more than declare two separate groups to be equally valued. Rather, the giving and receiving of hospitality among the people in this passage means new relationships form between those groups. What are the consequences? A new, unified community. Different people sharing kinship. Plenty of mutuality and salvation to go around.

Those consequences mean Cornelius's conversion cannot be considered private or "a personal matter." It will affect all the rest of Jesus's followers, for the centurion and his household now belong to their community. Their mere inclusion makes that community into a different kind of community. Hospitality entails a host making a commitment to a guest and honoring the guest's identity. For that commitment to be real, it must be demonstrated. Attitudes will have to adjust. Practices will have to expand or change. Strangers will have to be greeted. Customs will evolve.

God's intrusive activity involves much more than helping Peter figure out what he's permitted to eat for his midafternoon snack. As a result of this particular disruption, the church will never be the same again.

Acts 12:1–19

Coming to Our Senses

There was no small commotion . . . over what had become of Peter. (Acts 12:18)

The book of Acts shows its flair for high adventure in many of its dramatic episodes, but perhaps the prison escape scenes generate the most thrills. On three separate occasions (see also 5:17–26 and 16:9–40), extraordinary events, obviously divinely directed, free Jesus's followers from incarceration. It appears God wants to make a statement every now and then.

Other ancient religions told stories about their heroes being delivered from custody, fetters, and locked doors by their god. Traditions about Dionysus, also known as Bacchus, a god of wine and ecstasy, and his followers provide notable examples. For instance, in a drama by the Athenian playwright Euripides (fifth century BCE) called *Bacchae*, an officer reports to the king that the god's adherents fled from their detention after their fetters fell from their feet and locked doors unbarred themselves. One Jewish legend about Moses has him walking out of a prison's wide-open doors, passing guards laid low by death and sleep as he goes.

All good spy novels need a double cross; it's practically a required piece of the espionage experience. Perhaps, similarly, every good religion needs in its books a story about humiliating powerful opponents through miraculous escapes. Ancient religions that found themselves under pressures from political authorities found benefits—including enjoyment and courage—in passing along stories about their deity's ability to confound and embarrass their persecutors and their deity's power over measures of quarantining the faithful. In the miraculous escapes from prison, Acts declares with a flourish that nothing can ultimately halt the preaching of the word of God. This preaching will persevere, as will God, despite any human authority's best efforts to overwhelm or deter it.

At the same time, the story told in Acts 12:1–19 has its share of defeat and risk. As thrilling a scene as it is, the threat of death winding through it makes it also a very dangerous one.

This chapter marks the only appearance of "King Herod" in Acts. There were many "Herods" during New Testament times, and keeping clear which is which is further complicated by their family tree's scandalously interwoven branches. The Herod of Acts 12 (also known as Herod Agrippa I) was a grandson of "Herod the Great," who is the Herod linked to Jesus's birth in Matthew 2:1–18 and Luke 1:5. Further, both of these are separate from the Herod who ruled Galilee during Jesus's lifetime (see Luke 3:1, 19; 9:7–9; 13:31–35; 23:6–12); that was Herod Antipas, one of Herod the Great's sons. As the New Testament sees it, the most significant family trait these men all shared was their willingness to use violence to oppose the will of God and God's messengers.

Prior to this scene, throughout chapters 8–11, Acts describes the growth of the church in places beyond Jerusalem. But this growth does not equal a promise of irresistible victory. The church will continue to imitate Jesus through its suffering just as much as in the vibrancy of its ministries.

Herod targets church members for violence and takes the life of "James, the brother of John." This James was one of the original twelve apostles whom Jesus chose (Luke 5:10; 6:13–16). Why would Herod engage in state-sponsored persecution? Presumably to weaken or destroy the church in Jerusalem by eliminating its leadership, a move that, Acts says, "pleased the Jews" (12:3). This statement cannot mean all Jews; after all, James, Peter, and most if not all the members of the Jerusalem church at this time are Jewish. Acts may be referring, rather, to only the Jewish leadership in the city, the aristocratic, temple-based officials who troubled the believers in Acts 4–5. At the same time, other recent indications of wider resistance within Jerusalem (Acts 6:9–12; 8:1; 9:28–30) suggest the church is now rankling even more people in the city, although Acts does not explain the reasons. Whatever the case, Peter finds himself next in line for martyrdom.

Herod clearly intends to exploit the political advantages he might gain by killing another apostle. We have seen this kind of thing before, for the setting is Passover (the Festival of Unleavened Bread), the time when Jesus was executed, but also the time when God once delivered the Hebrews from a tyrant's oppressive hand (Exodus 12). Fortunately for Peter, God intends a new exodus for him.

On the eve of his scheduled execution, as the church prays fervently for him, Peter experiences an amazing series of events. It seems like he is dreaming: an angel appears, chains fall off his arms, he appears invisible to multiple guards, and a heavy gate opens on its own. Once he finds himself alone and free, he comes to his senses and says the most sensible thing he can; ironically, it's a theological statement: God has done this (12:11). His confession is simple, but it has many predecessors in the Bible. Miriam and others responded similarly after the people of Israel escaped the Egyptians through the Red Sea (Exodus 15:19–21). Mary said essentially the same thing after learning of her pregnancy (Luke 1:46–55). These biblical figures view their experiences as theological events; they recognize God's presence in what they undergo. However Peter gets out of custody, he sees it as no accident. Luck or ingenuity cannot explain it; God is involved.

At that key point of realization, Peter has only moved *out* of incarceration. He has not yet been delivered *into* a place of security. First, he must get through one more passageway, and this one will not open miraculously. Getting through the locked gate outside the house occupied by Mary, the mother of John Mark, proves more difficult than getting out of his cell. It takes some time and persistence before Rhoda lets him inside. First, and with a note of exasperation or humor, she must persuade those praying fervently that their hopes have already been realized.

Finally, they open the gate and allow him entrance. Apparently, God and angels can do only so much for Peter. At the end, the church has to figure out what God has done and take action themselves. God doesn't take care of every door. The people of God have to open a few on their own. God's initiative makes Peter's safety *possible*. People, including Peter, have to make sure it actually comes to pass.

Peter recounts his adventure and instructs his companions to relay news of his deliverance to another James (probably one of Jesus's brothers, who emerges as a leader of the Jerusalem church according to Acts 15:13–21; 21:17–18) and others, but no time remains for celebration. Danger lingers, and Herod remains a threat. So Peter flees "to another place." We hear about him only once again in Acts, when he makes a cameo appearance at a church conference in chapter 15. God may have shown strength over Herod and frustrated his intentions, but Jesus's followers don't take their security for granted. Again, the people of God take action themselves.

The account of the prison escape concludes with one more statement of Herod's ruthlessness, when he has the prison guards executed for their dereliction of duty before he returns to his permanent residence in Caesarea, on the seacoast. With these deaths, the scene loses its capacity for comedy. It goes beyond being a slapstick account of a powerful God frustrating a futile king. People lose their lives. Tyrants will be tyrants, and their opposition to the will of God leaves a trail of destruction. Why does God not deliver the prison guards too? For that matter, why does James lose his life while Peter gets away? If God can rescue Peter, why doesn't God make all the persecution stop? We see the problems that grow out of reading too much into notions of God's providential care.

The spread of the gospel and the growth of the church do not remake the world into a safe—or fair—place. The miraculous intervention remains exactly that: miraculous, and therefore inexplicable and unexpected.

Acts does not ask us to turn the miracle into something normal or methodical. The escape does not give Peter the courage to mock Herod in public or to show up in the temple the next morning to deliver a public sermon. It does not restore him to a place where he can do exactly as he did before, yet it allows him to live out his witness to Jesus somewhere else. Peter has been the most prominent human character so far in Acts; after this he fades into places where the narrative will not venture. The story is ultimately about God and the work that Jesus passes along to his followers; it's not about these followers themselves or the church's need for heroic individuals.

If we keep the spectacular details from distracting us too much, we see this scene says much about recognition. Peter cannot quite wrap his head around what God is doing until the prison break is complete and he finds himself unchained and alone in the street. Rhoda and especially Peter's other associates initially do not recognize him, or they are too scared to believe the guy at the gate really is Peter. They remind us of disappointment's potential to leave scars: we might hope fervently for something, but it seems foolish for us to dare really to believe it will come to pass. Then we risk disappointment. Perhaps daring to recognize God's presence and influence in our lives, in ways either astounding or mundane, makes us confront the prospect of suffering letdown.

As with Peter, Cornelius, and company in Acts 10–11, recognizing God takes time and usually happens after the fact, when we have better perspective on a situation. We make and declare such recognitions with healthy doses of fear and uncertainty, acknowledging we may be disappointed in the end. We might be wrong. Circumstances might change. When the church in Mary's house opens the gate for Peter, they open themselves to the *possibility* of embracing a new or unexpected reality. They act more on a hunch than on settled confidence, on longing more than certainty. This is never easy. Our ability to take such steps depends much on who we imagine God to be. We gain more strength and courage if we believe that God delights in surprises or that God is willing to reorder our expectations into greater conformity with the gospel.

In contrast to everyone else in the scene, Rhoda, a character often overlooked, expresses openness to such things, and Acts subtly lauds her even as the others in the house initially dismiss her good sense. Do they resist her insight because she is just a slave? (And why on earth does a follower of Jesus still own a slave, anyway?) At least Rhoda's willingness to recognize that God might have done something, maybe even in response to the church's prayers, shows her theological perception to remain unfettered.

At least one person in this scene never comes to a point of recognition. This is Herod, who sets himself as an enemy to God's intentions. If we read on, to the end of Acts 12, Herod's story concludes in a nasty death when an angel of the Lord strikes him down because of his blasphemous arrogance. The struggle between God and Herod finishes with a clear statement: God wins.

Many of us long for a Christian life like this, in which good, faithful people like Peter escape all harm, and God's opponents receive their due. While this passage might promote those kinds of longings, it also foils them. True, the story of the miraculous deliverance and the dead oppressor proclaims that the gospel of Jesus Christ cannot ultimately be constrained. But the story of an executed James and a fugitive Peter reminds readers that, just as Jesus repeatedly promised in the Gospels, the life of discipleship involves struggle. At least it did when Acts was written, assuming that the book's ancient readers also sometimes suffered hardship or frustration in ways that might have struck them as potentially meaningless and patently unjust.

Our desire to sympathize with James and Peter may also expose our refusal to see how we resemble Herod: determined to squash our opponents, unwilling to acknowledge how others might be describing God in ways to which we are unaccustomed, too enamored with our own glory. This passage depicts a church that, on its own, possesses really very little power. It does what it can: it remains faithful, and it prays fervently. It must rely deeply on God. In today's Western societies, most of our churches operate a little differently.

I've seen established, respectable, twenty-first-century congregations of middle-class Christians struggle with the New Testament's images of vulnerable churches. Other kinds of congregations do too. Some of us, when faced with conflict and competing visions of what's possible, think it's up to us to rush in and fix everything. As a result, we sometimes respond more like Herod than like the prayerful believers in Mary's house. And the Rhodas in our midst, those who can actually see what's going on, still have a hard time getting our attention.

Road Map

God Is Still Speaking

Most of the action in Acts 1–12 involved Peter, along with a few other figures associated with the church located in Jerusalem. In Acts 13–28, Saul (who becomes known as Paul beginning in 13:9) occupies the narrative stage more than anyone else. When Peter had the spotlight, the action stayed confined to a relatively limited geographical area. Paul's ministry, conducted mostly in partnership with other disciples, covers much more ground. As the miles add up, readers observe Paul navigating a wide range of cultural landscapes.

With the exception of an important interlude in Acts 15, when the action quickly returns to Jerusalem, Acts 13–19 describes the representatives of the gospel journeying in areas inhabited predominantly by gentiles. These missionaries experience a spectrum of the eastern Roman Empire's cultural options, especially within some key cities.

Their excursions repeatedly call attention to what it looks like for the Christian message to become understandable in languages and categories people can grasp. Although there may be patterns and commonalities in what happens to Paul and his associates in these chapters, Acts does not present the gospel in a one-size-fits-all manner. Every destination has its particular culture, and bearing witness to God's salvation both attracts and disturbs people in light of those cultural realities. Repeatedly we see how disruptive the gospel can be: it may change how people think about God and the meaning of life, but it also alters core beliefs and practices connected to people's cultural and personal identities, their economic life, their political loyalties, their inherited wisdom, and their hopes for the future. In short, Acts gives reason to conclude that the good news about Jesus Christ leaves no aspect of a person's existence undisturbed.

No single story in Acts 13–19 offers enough detail to show fully how pervasive and disruptive the gospel can be in a particular place, but together these scenes call attention to enough facets of culture to draw a suggestive and composite sketch of what it entails for the word of God to speak to and take root within various cultural climates. As we will see, in each scene we benefit from learning more about the distinctive locations Paul and his partners visit. This permits us to attend to these places' cultural peculiarities with some of the knowledge ancient readers of Acts would have possessed. The information helps us appreciate the complexity involved in the story of Christianity's spread across and beyond the Roman Empire. It encourages us to reflect on how we hear and make sense of God's intentions in light of our own deeply embedded assumptions and categories—something we might also do with generosity and creativity as we consider what this gospel looks like from our neighbors' perspectives.

Acts 13:1–4

Called and Commissioned

> Then after fasting and praying they laid their hands on
> them and sent them off. (Acts 13:3)

Sometimes we don't want to be "sent off." An athlete ejected from
a game or a disruptive student dispatched to the principal's office
goes only because an authority demands it. On other occasions, anticipation and joy are part of the picture: we wave good-bye to loved
ones in airport terminals and dormitory parking lots to express our
excitement for imminent adventures. What's it like when God sends
us off to participate in something new?

When the Holy Spirit, in Acts 13, summons Barnabas and Saul
from the church in the Syrian city of Antioch and sends them off to
do "work," the Spirit's call includes a wider community. The larger
church acknowledges the Spirit's intentions and willingly relinquishes
these men. When these people send Barnabas and Saul away, they
willingly put themselves at the Spirit's disposal and declare that their
community exists not for its own sake; the whole community's calling is to participate in the unfolding realities set in motion through
God's good news.

In sending Barnabas and Saul off, this community does not cut
ties. Barnabas and Saul's associates in Antioch respond to the Spirit's
command with more than a statement of "So long, and good luck."

In 13:3 they act out the call from the Holy Spirit to "set apart" these two men. By laying hands on them, thereby calling upon God to be present in the moment, and dismissing them, the church gives them—and recommits itself—to the Spirit's power and oversight. All parties remain connected in this same, shared Spirit, no matter where Barnabas and Saul will end up.

Immediately, in the very next sentence, the storytelling alters our perspective on the occasion. When 13:4 begins, referring to Barnabas and Saul with the words "So, being sent out by the Holy Spirit, they went . . . ," the narrative conjures a very close association between the Antiochene church and the Holy Spirit. In 13:3 the church leadership sends ("they . . . sent them off"). The very next verse says the Holy Spirit does the sending ("being sent out by the Holy Spirit"). (In the original Greek, the "sending" verb in verse 4 is different from the verb in verse 3, although both carry the sense of propelling people on their way.) Acts makes it difficult to determine where one of these senders leaves off and the other begins.

Who sends Barnabas and Saul, then? The situation resembles what Saul learned on the road to Damascus, in Acts 9:5, when his persecution of Christians was equated to persecuting Jesus. As we know well by now, Acts is fond of describing God and the church in a very intertwined relationship. In 13:1–4, the sending by the church is the vehicle through which the Spirit sends. The Spirit initiates the process by issuing the call, but then the Spirit sends through the church's own act. The church does not merely imitate the Spirit's action; it performs it, serving as the means by which the Spirit works toward God's ends. It is a cooperative, integrated partnership.

Four short verses therefore invite readers to imagine the Holy Spirit connected to a community of Christian believers in two different respects. First, the Spirit stands separate from the local congregation, appointing people to be sent off under the Spirit's authority into new areas and tasks. Barnabas and Saul will eventually find themselves sent far away, beginning with a trip to the relatively nearby island of Cyprus. Second, the Spirit appoints by speaking and acting through the people who constitute the church, through the speech and activity of the congregation itself. How does the church know when it is doing this?

The close association between the Spirit's activity and churches' activity does not make the Spirit's voice simply reducible to the church's voice. Rather, as Acts portrays it, the church labors to ascertain the Spirit through its everyday life and its decision making. The active lines of communication between communities of believers and the Holy Spirit strike some modern readers as alien and others as dangerous. I have heard many churchgoers—and former churchgoers—recall occasions in which other Christians' reckless claims of knowing the will of God seemed a poorly disguised attempt to manipulate people or to squelch productive debate. These experiences have sometimes left Christians too scarred or sheepish to venture any suggestions about where or how the Holy Spirit might be stirring in their midst. Nevertheless, a scene like 13:1–4—along with others in which the Spirit provides guidance—exhorts communities of faith to look closely at their corporate lives and worship and at the needs of the wider world, to find indications of the Spirit's presence.

This renews the question: how does the church know when it hears the Spirit?

Acts never answers that question in clear or uniform ways. Do people in Antioch hear voices? Do they all come up with the same idea at once? We do not know. At the same time, the narrative's brief description of the church in Antioch might call attention to details that could help us understand what it means to be attentive to the Holy Spirit. One detail concerns the makeup of the church that seeks to respond to God's call.

Antioch—located close to the northernmost spot of the far-eastern edge of the Mediterranean Sea, near modern Turkey's border with Syria—figures in other parts of the narrative. Acts describes it as home to a thriving Christian community (11:19–30; 14:26–15:3; 15:22–35). In this passage, which names five people, we learn something about the church's composition. Like the population of many cities in the Roman Empire during the first century, people from many homelands and backgrounds resided in Antioch. The sizable array of cultural

identities is reflected in what we read about the prophets and teachers active in the Christian community there. Barnabas, a Jew, hails
from the island of Cyprus (see Acts 4:36). Saul is also a Jew (trained
as a Pharisee, he reports in Acts 22:3; 23:6; 26:5) who was born in
Tarsus, which sits very close to the southern edge of modern Turkey.
Given Simeon's nickname, Niger (meaning "black" in Latin), odds
suggest he is dark-skinned and African. Lucius's African origins are
even more certain since he hails from Cyrene, near the northernmost
point of modern Libya and directly south of Greece. Finally, Manaen,
whose familial history remains totally undisclosed, has some connection to the infamous Herodian family. The language allows for
multiple possibilities. Perhaps Manaen was a boyhood friend of one
of these rulers. Herod Antipas, the one who ruled Galilee during
Jesus's lifetime, appears to be the one meant. Or maybe Manaen
was a former member of a royal court, once an influential aristocrat
or bureaucrat. In any case, now in the Antiochene church, he rubs
elbows with leaders of a very different kind of enterprise.

The differences among these five men make their fellowship attract
our attention, since Acts rarely gives even this much personal detail
about characters. We can assume all of the five neither look nor sound
alike. Most likely, with a mixture of different complexions, different
cultural backgrounds, and different accents owing to different na-
tive languages or regions of origin, their gathering resonates with
the multicultural tones that marked the day of Pentecost, when the
Holy Spirit led Jesus's earliest followers to speak about God to Jews
and proselytes who originated from an extensive range of regions
(2:5–11). It appears Pentecost has had a significant effect: the presence
of God's Spirit has continued to call together people from all places.

While Acts speaks elsewhere of women who teach and possess
special prophetic gifts (18:26; 21:9), something hardly unusual in
early Christianity (according to, for one example, 1 Corinthians), we
may rightly wonder why none appear here. The variegated collection
of prophets and teachers in Antioch should not be overstated. No
women's names appear in the short list, thus reminding us of the ways
Acts often renders women and their contributions invisible. Whether
we attribute the description of an exclusively male cast of characters
to the influence of ancient cultural norms or to a biblical author's

agenda or ignorance, still we can justifiably argue that the attention given to the cultural or ethnic differences among the members of this church lends a warrant for affirming the importance of other forms of diversity in spiritual leadership.

Thus the Spirit speaks, or is heard, in a diverse collection of human beings. Differences among persons present no obstacle. Perhaps a complementary perspective also applies: we might question whether the Spirit has really been heard in occasions when everyone who claims to have heard already looks, talks, and believes exactly the same.

How might the diversity among the fellowship in Antioch make its members particularly attuned to see beyond themselves and be ready for the Spirit's call to send some of them away on God's behalf? The roster of leaders in Antioch keeps the broader world always visible. It reflects the gospel's wide scope and grand ambitions. It embodies Jesus's not-yet-completely-realized promise about the witness of his followers extending to the ends of the earth (1:8).

Another detail to note concerns the setting: the Spirit speaks to people in Antioch as they worship and fast. It's not clear whether the worshiping and fasting refer to the five leaders alone or also to other people in the Antiochene Christian community. In any case, the attention to worship should not surprise us, if we keep the whole story of Luke and Acts in view. The Holy Spirit descended upon Jesus as he prayed (Luke 3:21–22), and his appearance was transfigured while he prayed (Luke 9:28–29). Several familiar events in Acts connect prayer to the presence of the Holy Spirit and divine activity, including the practice of Jesus's followers in 1:14, the apostles' boldness in 4:31, the Spirit coming to Samaritans in 8:15–17, Saul's visit from Ananias in 9:9–17 (part of a larger passage that also mentions fasting), the vision given to Peter to lead him to Cornelius in 10:9, and a miraculous escape from prison as the prisoners pray and sing hymns to God in 16:25–26.

Worship, this passage implies, creates a context well suited for hearing the Spirit as a community together experiences and relives its memories, testimonies, service, shortcomings, hopes, and more. The people in Antioch don't worship out of a sense of obligation or to maintain their weekly rhythms. They worship because their lives have been turned upside down, and they seek to participate in the salvation God pledges to bring fully into being for them and the entire world. They live in response to God, ready to risk, so as to be a part of whatever is coming next.

Likewise worship, as a response to God, turns our attention outward—to consider God, to inquire of God, to embrace God's intentions for ourselves and for our neighbors, to wonder, and to make ourselves available. This scene does not indicate that worship *makes* the Spirit known or forces God to speak, but it suggests worship provides a fitting context for the Spirit to equip and motivate the people of a church. God's disruptions are not always accompanied by sights, sounds, and special effects. The story of the call of Barnabas and Saul commends a posture of eager expectancy and responsiveness in the course of a congregation's normal, regular life together.

Because nothing can be truly normal or regular anymore, not in a world after Pentecost.

Communal worship, where we meet to seek the face of God, is a good place to look and listen for God's Spirit. But our worship life can't allow us to get too comfortable with that Spirit. For in focusing our attention on God, we might find our routines disrupted and our friends or ourselves sent out to participate in God's desires to change the world, whether our first step takes us near or far away into that far-flung terrain.

Acts 14:8–20

Learning to Recognize God

He has not left himself without a witness in doing good.
(Acts 14:17)

Going to "the ends of the earth" involves more than travel. It also requires a good deal of translation as the gospel and its representatives move into different settings. It's a big earth, after all, and its peoples have lots of different ways of understanding things.

In Acts 14, we find Paul and Barnabas visiting various cities in Lycaonia, a region in the south-central area of modern Turkey, about a hundred miles away from the Mediterranean coastline. At this point in its history, Lycaonia was not exactly a hot spot for tourism. Ancient writers demeaned it as a backwater, off the beaten track and populated largely by superstitious yokels.

The account of Paul and Barnabas's time in a city named Lystra begins with mention of a man born with an impairment that has prevented him from ever walking. It sounds much like the opening verses of Acts 3, when Peter, fresh from his preaching debut at Pentecost, encountered a man with a similar condition in the temple. Paul commands the Lystran man to walk, and he does. Through this and other resemblances, Acts again steers us to see essential similarities between Peter and Paul. Both conduct the same ministry with the same God-given power to do so. It's a ministry inaugurated by Jesus, who himself healed a paralyzed man simply by commanding him to walk (Luke 5:17–26). Peter and Paul continue the ministry their Lord began; their work is nothing new, and it is not their own.

Jesus's healing in Luke 5 led to amazement from onlookers. Peter's did the same in Acts 3. Guess what happens in Acts 14? Indeed, a crowd of Lystrans responds excitedly. But they draw immediate theological conclusions in their excitement and decide that Paul and Barnabas are not ordinary mortals but deities visiting Lystra in human form. Apparently before Paul and Barnabas can realize what is going on—it doesn't seem to help that everyone's shouting in Lycaonian—a priest arrives on the scene with oxen fit for a sacrifice to the gods Zeus and Hermes. These people can't wait to act on their hasty religious reflexes.

Recall Lycaonia's ancient reputation as an abode of ignorant hicks. Add this reputation to the story in Acts, and there's something predictable, even hilarious, about the Lystrans' reaction. Acts does not describe why these people might witness a healing and then leap to conclusions about divine visitation. It looks like gullible superstition unleashed.

But before we assume this passage is just about playing with stereotypes so readers can wag their heads at those poor, silly Lystrans, there is more to consider.

Ovid, a Roman who wrote roughly a century prior to the composition of Acts, tells a story about this same region in his mythological poem *Metamorphoses*. He describes these same two gods, Zeus and Hermes (known as Jupiter and Mercury in Ovid's Latin), visiting this area disguised as human travelers. No one offers them hospitality or gives them food and drink except for a poor, elderly couple named Baucis and Philemon. Next, the gods reveal their true identities to the unsuspecting pair and reward them. A flood wipes out the region's other, selfish inhabitants.

It's a familiar tale: show hospitality because you might be entertaining gods or angels without knowing it. Its flip side should be familiar too: don't accidentally be rude to veiled deities or they might wipe you out in response.

We cannot be too sure about whether the legend preserved in Ovid's work occupied a large part of the cultural consciousness in Lycaonia, but it certainly figured in the ways many of the earliest readers of Acts would have understood this passage. The Lystrans' confusion about Paul and Barnabas, while retaining some of its comic qualities in the people's speedy response and the missionaries' temporary confusion about the crowd's intentions, makes a lot of sense. If part of their basic cultural memory involves a story about divine visitation and the mortal dangers associated with mishandling powerful deities, why shouldn't they be hastily careful to treat Paul and Barnabas with the greatest respect they can imagine? We can poke fun at their sensitivity and ignorance even as we empathize with their fear and resolve.

Paul and Barnabas have other things to worry about in the thick of this story. Entirely uneager to be acknowledged as gods who might need worship or appeasement, they tear their clothes to express their severe distress. In doing so they communicate they want no part of what is about to happen. This act, plus a very short speech, barely manages to foil the plan for a sacrificial ox roast.

Paul's three-verse-long speech hardly explains the full gospel. It never refers to Jesus but instead asks the Lystrans to consider evidence for a single, benevolent God. Rip the speech from its narrative setting, and it sounds rather unspecific and vague. When we consider the Lystrans' situation, however, we discover Paul trying to lay foundations for a depiction of God that could be particularly well suited and understandable to this specific audience. The speech teaches us about God, yet it also teaches us about how important our religious imaginations are and how they are shaped.

The speech centers on the notion of one, true God, "the living God," who creates and sustains everything. When Paul speaks of God allowing all people "to follow their own ways" in the past, he emphasizes the present time as the moment for God to be recognized. The focus from Pentecost continues: the time has now come for the salvation of "everyone who calls on the name of the Lord" (2:21). God was not indifferent or absent in the past, just detectable to the nations of the world in subtle yet vital ways. Always God provided "a witness" to vouch for God's benevolent care. The life-giving sustenance of the earth and its produce have provided such evidence.

Paul doesn't offer a reasoned argument *against* the Greek and Roman pantheons of deities. Nothing about his brief comments concerning nature's witness leads to the conclusion that one God makes more sense than multiple gods. Rather, his speech attends more to the question of how God might become manifest to humanity and what we might thus expect God to be like.

Tender images of Christmas and our belief in the coming of Jesus as an expression of God's love make it easy for us to overlook how utterly terrifying the notion of a deity directly entering into our lives can be. It all depends on the deity's personality, for one thing. In much Greek and Roman religion, the deities were beings to be avoided, appeased, or sought mostly when specific help was needed. When the ancient myths speak about gods or goddesses who take notice of human beings and enter their space, the outcomes are usually not good for the people involved.

The Lystrans, with their cultural memories about unappreciated gods circulating around the area and eventually destroying the place, live with acute awareness of the gods' capriciousness. Deities can be dangerous intruders, and a violent end might come to those who displease them. Paul's speech may strike the Lystrans as slightly peculiar, then, for its attention to the living God's goodness, a goodness discerned through the natural world. God sends the rains not to punish the wicked and ignorant with floodwaters but to feed everyone.

(Granted, Paul does not bring up the topic of Noah's ark, nor does he explain why nature's occasional fury can do as much to imperil human existence as it does to support it on good days. Those thorny topics need to wait for another day. He's just getting started with the Lystrans.)

Could fear—fear rooted deeply within their cultural memories and identities—motivate the Lystrans' desire to offer sacrifices to Paul and Barnabas? If so, it could explain why Paul ends his brief speech with mention of God's intention to fill "hearts with joy." It's not time to discuss Jesus's crucifixion and resurrection. First, these people need to confront the possibility that God has a deep, unwavering commitment to human flourishing and well-being.

God, then, is not just kind. God is the model of hospitality. God sustains and gives joy to all who live in this creation. At least that's how it's supposed to work.

A quick glance at the day's headlines reminds all of us that real life is hardly so rosy. Acts acknowledges this truth, perhaps, at the end of this account. The story does involve violence, but it comes from human beings. Paul and Barnabas's opponents from an earlier stop on their itinerary catch up with them and attack Paul, who escapes with his life through strange luck or a miracle. The missionaries will return to Lystra at a later time, although we do not learn what happens then (14:21). The beating Paul endures at the scene's end does not invalidate the theological vision he tries to impart to the Lystrans, but it does remind us that God's unbridled benevolence encounters resistance in humanity's bad behavior.

Acts might chuckle at the Lystrans' gullibility, and we easily perceive their superstitious worries and practices as odd or maybe primitive. But the caricature-heavy tone of this story can prompt us to consider our own culturally inherited blinders and expectations. I have known many people who live with assumptions about an angry, vengeful God who is barely able to hold back from punishing everyone right now. (These people can claim some biblical passages to support their view, but ultimately it misinterprets the Bible's overall depiction of God, I believe.) They did not manufacture this image of God out of thin air; it says something about how they were taught and how they think. Other people show no ability to imagine God as doing anything but supporting their determined pursuit of well-being and happiness. They have no thought that God might want them to alter their lifestyle or sacrifice their comforts for the sake of their neighbors in need. Still others presume God wants them to remain passive and accept their lot even as they suffer entrenched injustice or routine abuse. Where did all these assumptions come from, and how do they keep people unable to recognize the intentions of a generous and merciful God?

The point is not to suggest that only a select few of us possess a singular, true, uncontaminated understanding of God. Rather, our views about God have all been shaped by our (personal and communal) experiences; our past failings and successes stay with us. So too do our fears and hopes, past and present. Who we are, the cultures and families in which we circulate—these shape our religious imaginations, for better or for worse.

Acts understands this, and in its own way the book respects the complexity of the matter. Maybe the story of Paul and Barnabas in Lystra can only raise questions for us to contemplate. The consistent assurance declared throughout Acts is that God is eager to have the gospel take root in lives, societies, and shared cultural foundations. That will happen in various ways, but in the process the gospel will continue to push everyone involved to reimagine our expectations. We will understand in new ways who we are, how we belong (or don't belong), and what we stand for.

The scary thing—for some, the reassuring thing—is that the gospel may, in the end, very well claim every aspect of who we are and what our lives are about. After all, God intrudes into our assumptions in both disorienting and curative ways not because God enjoys mocking our ignorance but because God cares for us and is eager to fill our hearts with joy.

Acts 15:1–35

Discerning God

> For it has seemed good to the Holy Spirit and to us to
> impose on you no further burden. (Acts 15:28)

Getting a group to come to agreement or make a decision about a controversial topic is hard enough. Doing it in a religious setting can be terrifying.

In religious communities, people often fixate on what one particular member of the group might think about an issue, and they worry deeply about offending that member if they make the wrong decision. The problem is that member is God, and God does not speak up in meetings. At least not aloud. Not that I have heard.

Yet God's inaudibility and characteristic inscrutability do not hinder the people who deliberate and act upon a critical question in Acts 15.

Just when readers thought the story had shifted totally to Paul and the spread of the gospel into locations inhabited predominantly by gentiles, Acts 15 arrives. It arrives to revisit the question of how gentiles participate in God's salvation. Even though Acts 10:1–11:18 gave the impression that Jesus's followers in Jerusalem were fine with including gentiles in the family without conditions, Acts 15 reveals persistent worry about the issue.

Earlier in this book, in our exploration of Peter and Cornelius's meeting in Acts 10:1–11:18, I noted how the story's participants couldn't make sense of God's intentions until the story was over. Then debate ensued. Theology—reflections on God and how God can be known—always works like this. Theology is retrospective, looking back on things that transpired and on people's attempts to articulate what they think about God's presence or involvement. Theology done in the moment usually is very bad theology because it tends to operate with limited information.

Likewise, theology done in isolation is usually bad theology. Or it is incomplete theology because it tends to operate out of insular perspectives. Theology involves debate because it involves talking with others and weighing their opinions. It entails letting time pass and evaluating the wisdom and consequences of its proposals. It requires conversation and attending to input from multiple participants, which usually means disagreement, or at least uncertainty, is inevitable.

The debate that erupts in Acts 15 shouldn't cause excessive worry, then. Announcing the gospel to gentiles and not requiring them to abide by the law of Moses, also known as torah, was a monumental development bound to breed discomfort, worry, and backlash among some. Why? Because many Jews of the time considered torah observance a basic aspect of expressing allegiance to God and enjoying the benefits of God's graciousness.

The debate mentions circumcision, a rather indelible sign of one's commitment to the law. The practice would of course pertain to men, although women would be affected as they considered how to relate to their husbands and sons. The overarching issue, however, is obedience to torah, including dietary restrictions, Sabbath observance, and other practices. The people who go to Paul's base of operations, Antioch (in Syria), from Judea (the region in which Jerusalem resided) do not try to toss the gentile believers out of the church. They intend to make their salvation complete through having them follow the law of Moses. Additional believers in the Jerusalem church—who still identify as Pharisees, reflecting their deep embrace of torah—agree. They cannot imagine how something as foundational to their identity as law observance cannot be a precondition for gentiles' inclusion in the people of God.

Paul and others strenuously disagree.

The controversy arises not only because some people apparently remain unaware of, or unimpressed by, what Peter and his associates observed in Acts 10:44–48, when the Holy Spirit came to a centurion's household in Caesarea. The pro-torah crowd probably presses their position in response to the growing number of gentile believers, which began in 11:19–26 and continued in Acts 13–14. They expect these new believers to enjoy the benefits they see in law observance. The growth of the church, its transition into new locations and circumstances, is prompting its members to make sense of what is occurring and make decisions about how it will operate as it moves into the future.

Acts includes many similar occasions in which change occurs and people have to determine, with limited insight, the best course of action to pursue. Differences abound in these situations; the decisions rarely follow the same process twice. In one instance, which strikes many today as arbitrary or superstitious, Jesus's followers "cast lots" (something akin to rolling dice) to determine an apostle to replace Judas Iscariot in 1:21–26. Other times involve more ordinary problem solving without any hope for divine guidance or speculation about what God might desire, such as in 6:1–6, when the apostles decided to commission some people to make sure widows received food. Elsewhere, as we have seen in 13:1–4, people sensed God directing them. The good news, then, is that there is no set, foolproof procedure that must be followed in all settings. But that's also the bad news, since it means people are usually left to cooperation and their best shared wisdom to figure out how to make important choices. Some things do remain consistent, however: decisions have to be made, changes have to occur, and they can prove disruptive to settled convictions or established procedures.

God does not give a speech during the proceedings described in Acts 15. However, people involved in the council repeatedly describe God as an active agent in the stories they relate.

Peter retells his experience of meeting Cornelius, saying "God made a choice" for Peter to be involved. He names God as the One who gave the Holy Spirit to Cornelius and his household, cleansed their hearts, and "made no distinction" between them and Jesus's Jewish followers.

Barnabas and Paul describe their ministry among gentiles in terms of "all . . . that God had done through them."

James appears to be the leader of the assembly. He is obviously not the same James as the apostle who was murdered in 12:2; he appears to be, according to Galatians 1:19, one of Jesus's brothers (see also Acts 12:17; 21:18). To the assembly he reaffirms Peter's perspective: *God* intervened into Cornelius's life. He refers to Peter as "Simeon," which approximates the Hebrew equivalent of the Greek "Simon," Peter's given name (Luke 6:14), thereby underlining Peter's Jewish bona fides among torah-observant believers.

James also alludes to God's involvement when he refers to Scripture, citing a Greek version of Amos 9:11–12. He endorses what is taking place among gentiles who turn to embrace Jesus, saying these developments can be expressed in terms of God's promise that the restoration of Israel (as "the dwelling of David") will result in gentiles coming to "seek the Lord" alongside God's chosen people. The gentiles who have come into the church's orbit and who do not observe the law of Moses do not represent a violation of God's intentions. They instead confirm what James and the others already believe to be true: that in Jesus Christ God has restored, or begun to restore, the people of Israel's health and glory.

When a letter goes out to gentiles in churches located in Syria and Cilicia to the north, it boldly tells them the council's decision "seemed good to the Holy Spirit" as well as to the council's leaders.

This is one of those meetings in which people want to consider what God thinks about the issue. Or, it is one of those meetings in which people want to say they know what God thinks about the issue. In the end, usually only slight differences separate those two kinds of meetings.

We can read this passage and the discourse taking place within it as very heavy-handed. While Acts mentions "much debate," the narrative never quotes the losing side's speeches. It even gives the questionable impression, by speaking of "the consent of the whole church," that no one went home from the council angry. Winners get to write history, after all. But anyone who has ever sat with another person who was convinced that he or she knew what "seemed good to the Holy Spirit" on an issue has reason to be concerned about the confident ways in which the people in this story speak of God at work in their midst. This passage should not give license for people to speak carelessly about God and God's involvement. It should not become a means for letting people claim special insight into God's intentions for the purpose of overwhelming the minority opinion (or, for that matter, the majority opinion).

On the other hand, we can also read this passage more charitably, hoping that it speaks of a community that was humble in its theological deliberations and indeed willing to listen to all sides of a debate. Perhaps the people in the room lean forward in a sense of impending discovery as everyone shares their insights. Perhaps all in the conversation are, like Peter when he obediently made his way to Cornelius's house, open to being surprised. Most encouraging, perhaps, is the way the narrated speeches proceed. They are not complex arguments about theological principles. They are not barrages of biblical texts shot across the room.

Instead, the speeches are mostly storytelling.

Peter describes, in greatly encapsulated form, his encounter with Cornelius. Who knows how long Barnabas and Paul speak? But they give reports from the field, telling what they have seen, owning their experiences. Individuals' stories and perspectives matter. They provide a starting point for wondering where God might connect to the issues on the table. Scripture does not provide a trump card for declaring what *must* be so; James turns to the prophet Amos not as a knockout punch or proof text but as a way of giving expression to the theological hopes that connect to how he is interpreting the current circumstances. The discussion appears to be open to "the whole church" even though James makes the final decision, or at least proposes it, on the basis of how he hears the discussion panning out.

Also, the council concludes with a compromise. The gentile believers are asked to adhere to certain essentials: avoiding foods associated with ceremonies to other deities, sexual immorality, and foods prepared in certain ways. The rationale for this list goes unexplained, but it may stem from a desire to prevent the new gentile believers from straying into idolatrous practices, to promote certain and limited scruples seen by some as intrinsic to Jewish identity, or to prevent the gentile believers from indulging in specific behaviors that would most offend the torah-observant members of the wider Christian community.

Whatever the reasons behind them, the instructions weaken the revolutionary notion that gentiles participate fully in the people of God with no requirements to fulfill. Yet the instructions also underscore the need for all sides in this new community to take steps to avoid wounding one another and thereby eroding unity—a unity meant to express the theological understanding that God "has made no distinction" between the two groups of people.

Maybe it would be easier if God would just write the answer on the wall and leave no ambiguity. But then the members of the church might not own their decision. Without debate and reflection they might not deeply ingest the decision's implications for their understanding of God and what it means for all of them to belong to God's people. The whole church, including its gentile newcomers, might forget that faithful living is about being in a dynamic relationship with a living God and with one another. Being in relationships like these takes work.

The conference is therefore not finally about winning an argument, crafting an effective strategic plan, refining customs, or making prudent judgments. The conference is about doing theology. The decision hinges on the council's ability to articulate *what it believes*, how it should interpret the things that have taken place over the course of the church's recent efforts to bear witness to Jesus. Discernment among Jesus's followers involves considering who God is, what God intends for the world, and how those things align with what the church experiences as it bears witness about Jesus. To consider these things is to make statements of faith, and the best statements of faith are those generated by communities in search of God through conversation with themselves, their traditions, and their lived experiences.

The sheer amount of attention given to this issue in Acts, here and in 10:1–11:18, suggests the issue is important and that its resolution does not come easily. The difficulty comes from the conversation but also from the challenges of living out one's theology. Acts acknowledges all these complexities. Lest we hastily think the book presents unity as a simple accomplishment, immediately after the letter from Jerusalem gets to Antioch we see unity fractured when Barnabas and Paul end their partnership over a disagreement (15:36–40).

In all cases, the conversations we undertake to reach theological conclusions and to embody the gospel carry risk. Temptations to assert God-given authority as a tool for manipulating others or to claim a victim's status always circulate among us. But the whole story of Acts encourages its readers to engage in such conversations anyway. Why? Because, like the citizens of Antioch and a thousand other cities, other people need Jesus's followers to devote serious, imaginative attention to articulating the character and consequences of God's salvation.

As churches do this vital work, they train themselves to remain always open to surprise and always keen to any new frontiers toward which God could be gravitating.

Road Map

Very Public Disturbances

Before venturing into Acts 16–19, recall the first two chapters of the story.

Jesus's followers departed from his ascension and, for several days, led a quiet existence of waiting for God to send power upon them. The Holy Spirit's arrival compelled them outdoors to speak. Then their lives and the witness they gave became public, visible to others. Even the more inwardly directed elements of the church's life—its worship, teaching, and service—nevertheless made an impression on the wider population (2:47). Acts consistently presents the gospel— the preaching of the word of God and the effects this word has on individuals and communities—as a very public thing. Sometimes people hear the word and respond to it in private settings, but later consequences become public and visible, such as when the Holy Spirit breaks onto the scene or when developments among some believers have ramifications for others and the unity of the larger church (as in Acts 10–11 and Acts 15).

Public things make statements to others. What's public can be scrutinized by others. For example, as Paul and his companions travel in various places throughout Acts 13–19, their audiences respond publicly to what they see and hear, such as the Lystrans when they mistake Paul and Barnabas for gods in 14:8–20. When people bear witness to Jesus through actions or words, it occasionally proves

disruptive, because the visible, public character of their activity provokes a response. Sometimes backlash results too.

Several scenes in Acts 16–19 include backlash, as people in well-
known cities publicly accuse Paul and his companions of acting dis-
ruptively or disseminating menacing ideas. The accusations often pose
serious consequences, and powerful people get involved. Together,
these scenes portray the gospel's ability to cause offense and generate
resistance because it can touch the raw nerves of foundational cultural
values. Exploring the nature and motives of this resistance helps us
better understand what the gospel is and how people in Acts experience it when Paul and others arrive in their neighborhoods. We can
also understand more of who God is when we observe how people in
Acts respond to declarations about God's intentions for the world.

The theological vision on display in Acts 16–19 derives more from
action than from speeches, as these chapters do not include many of
the latter. Moreover, most of the noteworthy action focuses on the
mischief of others and not on the deeds of Jesus's followers. In the
chapters to come, pay attention to what people fear. Those fears offer
insight into their sense of what might be disrupted if the gospel takes
root in their setting and has a widespread, public influence on how
others there choose to live. A similar point can be made concerning
the things they ignore or dismiss: how does ignorance or confusion
about aspects of Paul's activity and message reveal people's misunderstanding or discomfort about God's intentions?

Acts 16:9–40

Battle of the Gods

These men are slaves of the Most High God, who proclaim
to you a way of salvation. (Acts 16:17)

Perhaps the most contentious of the confrontational scenes in Acts
16–19 is the first one, which occurs in Philippi. It's a showdown over
who's ultimately in charge of things.

As soon as the conference in Jerusalem concludes in Acts 15, the
narrative again follows Paul and his associates who, after delivering
news of the meeting to Christians in Antioch, make their way into
Asia Minor (modern Turkey). Paul travels with Silas, Timothy, and
possibly others, as indicated by the narrator's peculiar shift from
third-personal narration ("*They* went," etc.) to first-person-plural
narration ("God called *us*," etc.) in 16:10–17.

Somehow the Holy Spirit deters the group from ministering in
Asia and Bithynia (a region in the northwest of what is now Turkey),
but then Paul has a vision of a Macedonian asking for help, which
everyone interprets as a sign of God's desire for them to preach in
Macedonia, north of Greece. They arrive in a city called Philippi.

Philippi sat on the Egnatian Way, a strategic east-west Roman
trade route. It gave access to the Aegean Sea and was surrounded by
good farmland and valuable minerals. Its identity as a Roman colony
distinguished it from ordinary cities. The Roman Empire organized

its colonies as distinctive places, making sure they maintained close cultural ties to Rome so as to cultivate a very Roman ethos in each place. Philippi's colonial legacy was significant, due to its proximity to the site where in 42 BCE Octavian (who became Augustus, the first Roman emperor) and Antony vanquished two ringleaders in Julius Caesar's assassination, Cassius and Brutus. When Octavian later settled many of his soldiers in Philippi, the city's importance increased. After Octavian consolidated his power by defeating the forces of Antony and Cleopatra at Actium in 30 BCE, he sent additional colonists to Philippi and added his own name to the city's official name: Colonia Iulia Augusta Philippensis.

When Paul arrived in the colony—nearly a century after that history—the place still was deeply identified with explicitly Roman values and power. When a flea landed on Rome, Philippi scratched itself.

Paul and company's first encounter with someone in Philippi, however, occurs outside the city walls when he meets a woman who hails from Thyatira, across the Aegean Sea. The woman is Lydia, and her home, Thyatira, sits in a region named Lydia. Perhaps she's named after her birthplace. Perhaps it's a nickname. Perhaps people in Philippi call her Lydia so no one forgets her status as a foreigner or outsider. The meeting place is "a place of prayer," an appointed gathering spot for Jews and others who might be inclined toward the God of Israel (which Lydia seems to be, as "a worshiper of God"). Lydia is a businesswoman in her own right. She enjoys enough wealth, status, or family to possess a "household" of her own made up of relatives, slaves, business subordinates, or perhaps a combination thereof. Acts mentions no father, husband, or sons. All she has is *hers*.

Following the conversion and baptism of her entire household (for at that time, the religious identity of all members of a household was determined or strongly influenced by the head of the household), Lydia provides hospitality to the traveling missionaries. All these relative outsiders to Philippian society find one another outside the walls and form the city's fledgling Christian community. We know nothing else about this Lydia, but Acts immortalizes her as the first convert in the mission to Macedonia.

Another woman then enters the narrative's spotlight. Acts does not divulge her name, but she is a slave with a very lucrative talent. Or gift. Or curse. The woman possesses "a spirit of divination," giving her clairvoyant abilities. Literally, Acts says she has a "Python spirit," probably indicating the spirit's association to Apollo, the god who, according to his mythology, killed the Python of the famed oracle at Delphi and thereby gained the power of divination. Apollo also had been one of Augustus's favorite deities, one the emperor sometimes proudly associated with himself.

The action happens quickly. The slave continually announces to all who can hear what Paul and his associates are doing in Philippi. Although she technically speaks the truth, for some reason it perturbs Paul, who easily demonstrates the power of Jesus's name over the spirit and dispatches it. What grates on Paul? He may be picking a fight, eagerly desiring to offend and embarrass anyone who wants to delight too much in Apollo, in the god's importance as a symbol of Roman or Augustan might, or in the idea of fortune-telling. It's also possible that Paul wants to be introduced to the public with more than a technically true statement about him, Silas, and their purpose for coming to the colony. For a statement about the salvation he and Silas preach to be *authentic*, it should come from one who bears and embodies the gospel. Jesus may have silenced demons who spoke the truth about him for similar reasons (see Luke 4:31–35).

We never learn what happens to the woman. Without the spirit, she becomes another ordinary slave, a piece of property now worth much, much less to her aggrieved owners. We can wonder if she could find sanctuary and new belonging in Lydia's house, but nothing in the narrative feeds this hope. In any case, the action continues without her: the woman's owners bring action against Paul and Silas, although the connection between their accusation and the missionaries' deeds is confusing. Their complaint does not focus on economics, the damage done to their property. It's an uglier charge, targeting Paul and Silas as "Jews" who advocate "customs that are not lawful for us as Romans to adopt or observe." Although their claim could reflect an innocent misunderstanding of the gospel that these Jewish men preach, instead it appears designed to stoke resentment against any attempts to diminish Roman superiority and perhaps resentment against Judaism itself. Judaism was not illegal, nor was Christianity when it emerged as an identifiable movement within and later distinct from Judaism. The angry slave owners appeal rather to cultural pride and prerogative. They want the local magistrates and gathered crowd to view Paul's expulsion of the Python spirit as an assault against Roman identity and values.

The magistrates publicly humiliate Silas and Paul, stripping them naked and beating them before placing them, chained, in a cell deep within a building. The spectacle appears designed to discredit the men along with their message, and also to demonstrate the colony's control—thus, by extension, Rome's control—over them.

Twice already in Acts (5:17–26 and 12:1–19), incarceration has meant miraculous deliverance, and God does not disappoint in Philippi. Somehow an earthquake opens doors and unfastens chains without bringing the roof down on everyone's head. The account may have sounded familiar to ancient audiences who knew an older tale told by Euripides about the deity Dionysus, in which the god, disguised as a human being, escapes custody when an earthquake breaks his fetters. Here in Acts, of course, the ones incarcerated are not God.

After the earthquake, the jailer, concluding his life is forfeit for having lost all his prisoners, prepares to kill himself when Paul stops him. The jailer's question, "What must I do to be saved?," carries a delicious double meaning. He wants to know how he can survive every prison guard's worst nightmare with his life intact, but Paul and Silas speak of a different kind of salvation. Within minutes, the one who locked up the missionaries hosts them in his house.

Acts does not explain why the magistrates order Paul and Silas's release the following morning, but one could assume the earthquake convinces them to stop playing games about who can control whom. The best way for Philippi to save face at this stage would be for Paul and Silas to leave quietly. Paul, however, will not stand for this. His public shaming warrants a public restoration, and he won't leave the wrecked prison without an apology and a public gesture. Paul wants no one to assume he and Silas escaped. Even more, he wants no one to miss the officials' acknowledgment of his God's power; no human authority can restrict the activity and influence of these "slaves of the Most High God," as the slave with the Python spirit called them. Paul wants the magistrates to concede openly, in full view, the futility of their opposition to what God is doing through Silas and Paul, as if the opened prison building doesn't already make this point terribly obvious.

Paul, now countering the original charges against them, declares that he and Silas are Romans. If he means they possess legal status as Roman citizens, this would greatly aid their case. Only a small percentage of people in the Roman Empire held this status at this point in history. (In fact, some scholars wonder whether the real Paul actually could have been a citizen. He never mentions it in the letters he wrote that appear in the New Testament. He also claims, in Acts 21:39, to be a citizen of the city of Tarsus. To be a citizen of both Tarsus and Rome would put Paul within the most elite stratum of the governing families in the eastern Roman Empire during the first century. Not impossible, but not likely.) Paul's claim to citizenship raises eyebrows because it afforded certain rights. Those with this legal standing were not supposed to be bound or subjected to corporal punishment and torture. Who's guilty of violating anti-Roman laws and ideals now? The magistrates could land in hot water for what they have done. Paul's retort adds one more embarrassment to the colony in its encounter with Paul and Silas: two men accused of endangering Roman values declare themselves to be loyal Romans, perhaps with significant social status.

Back in 5:41, after Peter and other apostles were detained and flogged in Jerusalem by the high priest and his advisers, "they rejoiced that they were considered worthy to suffer dishonor for the sake of the name."

Paul does not share this perspective in Acts 16.

At least he doesn't share it as the scene ends. A little earlier, as he and Silas sing hymns in their prison cell still smarting from the torture inflicted on them, maybe then he's rejoicing. Why all the chest thumping when the magistrates want to release them?

It's because this scene depicts a contest and struggle over power. Not Paul's power and rights versus the magistrates', but God's power vis-à-vis Rome and the all-encompassing claims of the gospel vis-à-vis Roman pride and privilege. The purpose of the earthquake is not escape but vindication. It asserts authority. It declares a winner.

The narrator keeps ambiguous what it might mean to call Paul and Silas's words and actions anti-Roman, as the slave owners assert they are. Paul and friends do not come to Philippi to overthrow Rome or spit in the face of Roman culture. But the gospel does have implications for Roman values and assumptions about imperial power. From this point forward, Acts will explore some of those implications through stories of Paul's adventures and the backlash against him.

As the magistrates suffer humiliation next to their gutted prison structure, Acts implies that Paul and Silas's ministry, because God directs and endorses it, cannot ultimately be thwarted by obstacles put in its way by individuals, governments, societies, or bald imperial pretentiousness. If those things position themselves in the way of God's designs, God reserves the right to overturn them. Jesus's followers are not immune to setbacks in Acts, but sometimes in the narrative God just makes a statement. This is a loud one.

Taken to an extreme, behavior like this could paint God as coercive and peevish. In this instance, maybe it merely means that God doesn't want certain rivals to presume they know better. After all, some cultures need more of a kick in the pants than others to get over their arrogant presumptions and their love of power.

Acts 17:16–34

The Gospel in the Flesh

Athenians, I see how extremely religious you are in every
way. (Acts 17:22)

Only rarely in Acts do people travel to hear the gospel message. For
the most part, the message about Jesus Christ comes to them, borne
by messengers. This illustrates an important truth about this gospel: it
meets people where they are—in their settings, usually with language
or concepts that make sense to their particular circumstances. It even
meets people in their own selves. Paul's speech in Athens provides a
remarkable statement about God's willingness to intrude quite close
to our existence, to meet us in our own flesh.

A few decades ago, people who study Acts for a living tended to
emphasize the book's speeches or sermons—there are between twenty-
four and twenty-eight of them, depending on how you count—as
the places where Acts makes its most important claims about who
God is and how God operates. That view has mostly passed away by
now, not because anyone thinks the speeches do not describe God but
because other parts of Acts—the narrative as a whole—do much to
depict God and God's activity. That is, the speeches have no special
claim over other passages as better or richer sources for insight into
who the book understands God to be. Accordingly, so far in this
book I have skipped over several of the speeches, preferring instead

to investigate how God figures into dimensions of the story's action. But the speech Paul gives in Athens is too good to pass up.

For many readers, the speeches in Acts appear repetitive. For one thing, most are concerned with telling audiences about God and what God has done, specifically in light of Jesus's death and resurrection. On closer examination, however, the speeches show their individuality. Each one fits its setting, so to speak. The emphases and perspectives in Paul's sermons to gentile audiences differ greatly from, for example, Peter's words to Jewish listeners in Acts 2–3. Peter offers his audience ample references to the Jewish scriptures (Christians' "Old Testament"), while Paul's arguments usually proceed differently. Remember when Paul and Barnabas pleaded with the people of Lystra (14:8–18), a population reputed to be unsophisticated and given to silly superstitions, at least according to stereotypes others held about them? Paul and Barnabas appealed to the reliability of the weather and seasons to support their case. In Acts 17, however, Paul finds himself in a very different cultural setting: Athens. So he quotes famous dead poets and discusses humanity's myriad ways of groping to find the divine in the natural world. His audience represents, at least in their own minds, the heights of intellectual sophistication in the Greek-speaking world. We might compare the situation with what it would be like for a twenty-first-century Paul having a chance to give a speech in the middle of Harvard Yard or at a Mensa conference.

No wonder Acts seems to relish the chance to tell this story. Ancient historians described Athenians as extremely intellectually curious and Athens as a very religious place. Acts does much of the same when it says, tongue buried deeply in cheek, that Athenians "spend their time in nothing but telling or hearing something new." These people are obsessed with ideas, especially novel and startling ones. Even more amusing, Paul apparently has not traveled to Athens in search of converts. Because of trouble in Thessalonica and Beroea (17:1–15), he had to flee and now waits for Silas and Timothy to catch up with him in the famous city. But the local religious climate proves too much for him to handle. He cannot wait in obscurity but loses his composure: "deeply distressed" by all the religious shrines and statues scattered throughout Athens, his restraint evaporates. He begins discussions with Jews and other worshipers in synagogues, as well as with any gentiles he can collar each day in the marketplace. Eventually, a gaggle of intellectuals (or they may be posers, since the narrative leaves us wondering how much to respect them) gets excited. One portion of them dismisses Paul as a "babbler," a philosophical hack who scavenges bits of ideas with no ability to put them together into a meaningful whole. Others, always eager to discuss new things, recognize his message as claims concerning divinities from a distant land—someone called "Jesus" and perhaps another god named "Resurrection." These really smart people are close to getting it, but still they need help with the details.

Fortunately, they have a plan. They usher Paul to the Areopagus, where he can make his case before a larger and more distinguished audience. "Areopagus" literally means "Mars Rock" or "Mars Hill," which was the place where Athenians in earlier centuries adjudicated court cases. Things had changed by Paul's time, and so Acts probably refers not to the hill but to the official body named after that place: the Areopagite Council, the city's governing authorities. Nothing suggests Paul has legal trouble. Instead, the zealous crowd wants the city's most powerful people to hear what he has to say. Without much effort on Paul's part—and again perhaps we're supposed to grin as we read this—he finds himself facing an ancient equivalent of the Harvard University faculty and fellows. This distinguished group politely asks him to explain his "strange" new religious message. An opportunity too good to be true! The gospel has found its way to the intellectual elite!

The scene therefore has a bit of a *Mr. Smith Goes to Washington* charm and one-upmanship about it. How did little old Paul end up here, addressing such an august group and exposing their ignorance? Amazing! But a more serious spirit of accomplishment and victory also fills the air: the message about Jesus—the word of God—will always find an audience, no matter how noble or inaccessible a segment of the population seems to be. Furthermore, the gospel will speak that audience's language; it will find common ground with some of the audience's basic assumptions, even if it might yet reveal their shortsightedness in the process.

The God of Jesus Christ therefore has as much to do with Athens as with Jerusalem. The word of God *belongs* in this place, as well as in every other one. (And, sorry to spoil the ending, this God will also eventually be proclaimed in Rome, the center of the empire, before Acts draws to a close.)

Paul does not disappoint; his speech indicates he understands his Athenian listeners well.

He begins with an effective hook: he has seen an altar in Athens dedicated to "an unknown god." Perhaps the Athenians have recognized that there is more to divinity than their many religious systems can capture. Their religious fervor has not closed them off to the possibility that contemplating the gods (or God) may finally involve more than what human insight can comprehend on its own. Paul declares he has "an unknown God" he wants to introduce to them. Next, he quickly establishes common ground by pointing out the absurdity of imagining that gods live inside manufactured things, like statues, altars, and temples. (Stephen made a similar point to a Jewish audience, back in 7:48.) The religious symbols, rituals, and objects we devise can never capture or fully represent God. The Athenians know this; their altar to a yet unknown deity shows they understand the limits of their knowledge and religious inquiries.

Where, then, do we discover God, if not in the holy things we construct and gather around? Paul steers attention toward human existence and the natural order. In these places God beckons humanity to search for God. In these places God may be found. Says who? Greek poets, that's who. The line "In him we live and move and have our being" was probably first written by Epimenides (sixth century BCE), and "For we too are his offspring" likely comes from Aratus (third century BCE). We are nearer to God than we might realize. Or maybe it is more accurate to say that God is nearer to us, dwelling among us and reaching out to us.

Probably no one in his audience takes much offense at anything Paul says up to the end of 17:29. For the most part, his claims would have sounded sensible, or at least within the ballpark, to his audience. Acts mentions the presence of Epicurean and Stoic philosophers in

Athens. Although these groups did not agree on many things, both looked to the natural world as a source of knowledge about life and meaning. For Stoics, a well-lived life involved seeking to know and align oneself with the divine will, which gives structure to the world and its operations. Epicureans, by contrast, saw less purpose woven into the universe and no opportunity for humans to connect with deities; for them, matter was not the creation of any divine being.

The speech changes when Paul moves to the particularity of God's nearness to us—what this accessibility looks like and how we discover it. Paul roots the ideas of repentance and judgment in the resurrection of Jesus (although he never mentions the name *Jesus* in the entire speech to the council). At this point, with his reference to Jesus's resurrection and the implication that all people will likewise be raised from the dead, Paul departs from most Athenians' basic notions of what it might look like to experience communion with the Divine. A large percentage of the crowd, being Greek, probably held to an idea of an immortal soul that at death finally escapes the limitations imposed by the human body. (Stoics, however, generally preferred to leave the details about postmortem existence unresolved or undefined. As for Epicureans, they mostly rejected any suggestion that life continues after death, even for the soul.) Greeks had various beliefs concerning the afterlife, but Paul offers a different perspective, rooted in a specific man, Jesus.

The idea of a God who brings bodies back to life appears to be too much for some within the Areopagite Council to hear, and so the speech is interrupted, which is how most speeches in Acts end. The audience divides into three groups: scoffers, those willing to hear more, and a number of men and women who believe what Paul proclaims.

In this speech, Paul cannot adequately explain the God he has encountered in Jesus Christ in general terms alone, by focusing only on human reason and our experience with the natural world. He must move into particularity, the ways God can be grasped in a man who was "appointed" and raised "from the dead" (17:31). In this man, Paul insists, the God of all creation comes near to us, among us. The gospel, for all of its lofty claims, remains very "fleshy": God's salvation came to us in Jesus's body and bears promises for the future of our own bodies. God does not aspire to remain "an unknown god"; Jesus, in nearness—in an embodied life, death, and resurrection—discloses this God to us.

Paul's speech underscores at least two important points about the gospel as a message about God and God's activity on humanity's behalf. First, it reminds us that salvation doesn't exist in some pure, unadulterated form with no connection to human languages, cultures, and our foundational assumptions about the world. Paul preaches an enfleshed message: one enfleshed in the Athenians' religious curiosity, one able to build on common ground Paul recognizes between his and his audience's convictions. God may disrupt or confound our preexisting understanding of what's valuable or possible just as Paul's comments about resurrection disturb many in his audience. But the message of God's good news also connects to what we hope for and what we know, whether we are like the Athenians, the Lystrans, or any number of other groups trying to figure out what life is all about.

Second, Paul's speech spotlights resurrected life as a core piece of Christian hope. The Easter message is about more than God undoing Jesus's death; it is about a promise God makes to us in Jesus. God promises to change us; God's judgment will result in righteousness, restored relationship between humanity and God. Jesus's resurrection indicates this relationship should not be understood as merely a spiritual recognition or a totally unrecognizable kind of existence. It's a relationship that involves bodies. Resurrected, remade, changed bodies, yes, but bodies nevertheless.

God, like the gospel, is fleshy. God values our embodied selves and intends a future for them. What dignity this ascribes to our existence—mine, yours, and all our neighbors'. What importance it lends to our efforts to discover God in all our interactions with one another.

Acts 18:1–17

When the Good News Escapes Attention

Speak and do not be silent; . . . there are many in this city who are my people. (Acts 18:9–10)

You could find many different kinds of people in ancient Corinth. It was a place for making connections.

Corinth sat near Paul's previous location, Athens. Fewer than forty miles separated the two places. Because Corinth rested on a narrow isthmus, overland traffic between southern and northern Greece ran through or near the city. Two miles from a port on a gulf to the north and four miles northwest of a port on a different gulf, Corinth also saw a lot of sea traffic, for some cargo could be transported across the isthmus to avoid a longer sea voyage around the southern end of Greece. As a result, the city was a crossroads for industry, shipping, commerce, and culture. Culturally vibrant and at times raucous, Corinth had seen various people groups and religions take root in its soil. Not surprisingly, then, this brief passage from Acts recognizes the variety and tells of disputes that can arise when diverse populations with diverse religious beliefs reside in close quarters.

Paul teams up with a couple who also count themselves among Jesus's followers: Aquila, a fellow Jew, and his wife, Priscilla. Aquila

hails from Pontus, a region along the Black Sea in what is now northern Turkey, although he and his wife recently came to Corinth from
Rome because they were among a group of Jews expelled from the
city by the Roman emperor Claudius. Eventually Paul's companions
Silas and Timothy arrive; they had separated from Paul in Beroea,
almost two hundred miles to the north, in 17:10–15.

Once everyone connects with each other, Paul has already been busy
speaking about Jesus to whoever listens—Jewish audiences gathered
in synagogues for learning, worship, and civic activities, as well as
groups of gentiles in other settings. When a particular gathering of
Jews resists his message and insults him, however, he shakes his clothing to dissociate himself from them (a gesture of similar symbolism
occurs in Nehemiah 5:13). Then he tells them (imitating, perhaps,
the words of the prophet in Ezekiel 33:4) he can do nothing more
to help them and so they bear full responsibility for their ignorance
and its consequences.

Paul's sharp words mark a turning point for the ministry he conducts in Corinth; the local Jewish audience has made him so upset
he declares he will henceforth devote his energy to the gentiles in the
city, presumably only to the gentiles. The outburst does not mean
he abandons his Jewish neighbors or his own identity as a Jew; it
means he changes his base of operations in Corinth. He doesn't
move far, finally, as he relocates this base from the synagogue to the
house next door.

Paul has played this card before. Back in Antioch of Pisidia, he
and Barnabas responded similarly to opposition from a Jewish crowd
(13:45–46), declaring they would go to gentiles. At their very next destination, however, the pair began their ministry in Iconium by speaking in a Jewish synagogue (14:1). Apparently they swiftly changed
their minds, or their frustration applied only to one particular group
of Jews. History will repeat itself when Paul eventually leaves Corinth.
When he gets to Ephesus as soon as 18:19, the first thing he will do
is visit a synagogue to talk to Jewish residents. This pattern should
make us hesitant to ascribe too much finality to Paul's "I'm finished
with you" eruptions, including the final one coming in 28:25–28.

Although Paul's turn from Jews to gentiles in 18:6 changes the
course of his Corinthian ministry, nevertheless his preaching finds

success among the synagogue members. Crispus, a synagogue leader, puts his faith in Jesus, as does his wider household. Gentiles respond similarly, including Titius Justus, who was already worshiping the God of Israel and whose house becomes the new locus of Paul's ministry, along with "many of the Corinthians."

The positive reactions to Paul's ministry make it difficult to understand why he receives a vision of Jesus Christ at this point in the story. Is he planning to leave for another city? Is he fearful in response to the opposition he has encountered? Most likely the vision encourages Paul to commit himself to Corinth for an extended time, for Acts subsequently notes he remains in the city a full eighteen months, probably so he will encounter, preach to, and teach the "many in this city who are [Jesus's] people."

We never learn who these "many" are, or their number. Also, the narrative does not explicitly say whether Paul himself ever locates them or identifies who they are. This may strike readers as surprising given all the other places in the book where Acts joyfully reports numbers and expansion (such as 2:41; 4:4; 6:7; 9:31; 12:24; 19:20; 21:20).

If we nevertheless trust Paul's vision, the "many" are out there, somewhere in this pulsing city. Perhaps they already follow Jesus. If so, it would not be out of line with other places in Acts where believers emerge from unseen places without any indication of how they came to follow Jesus. In 28:15, for example, believers from Rome will meet Paul before he even reaches the city. The churches in Acts do not always need apostles or other celebrity preachers for growth to occur; others bear witness to Jesus, and so Jesus himself certainly remains active, even if far from the narrative spotlight. Don't assume Acts tells *the* story, the *whole* story, or the *only* story.

The God of Acts can be full of surprises. This God is working out other stories, finding and calling people in ways and places you have not thought to look into yet.

Eventually a public outcry develops, similar to other scenes scattered throughout Acts 16–19. As these confrontations go, the one in Corinth starts out fairly orderly.

An unknown but apparently organized group of Jews—unknown because Acts lazily refers to them as only "the Jews"—brings Paul to court. The tribunal in Corinth sat in the middle of the marketplace, a very visible place. Gallio, who was governor (technically, proconsul) of the wider province that included Corinth, hears the charge.

The scene quickly turns as confusing as it is brief, for key developments go unexplained. Paul's Jewish prosecutors claim he violates the law in his ministry because of how he induces or persuades people to turn to God. Which law is it—Roman law or the law of Moses that governs Jewish faith and practice? Probably they mean the former, for a Roman governor would have little interest in hearing about the latter. The charge, then, echoes the ones against Paul and Silas in Philippi, that somehow the gospel undermines and imperils Roman values (16:20–21). The accusation is weak, and without any controversy attending it (like the lost value of the Philippian slave girl), it fails to generate any heat.

Paul does not even get to answer the accusation, for Gallio does not agree and refuses to hear more. Perhaps he sees everything clearly and considers the charges specious. Perhaps he dislikes the accusers and delights in embarrassing them; he would be neither the first nor the last Roman official to treat Jewish subjects dismissively. Perhaps the governor is too busy or careless to investigate the claims and implications of this new Christian teaching. In any case, Gallio regards the case as about differences of opinion pertaining to the law of Moses, not to Roman law, since no "crime or serious villainy" seems to be involved. Beyond that, he simply does not care.

Gallio's callousness intensifies as the scene comes to an odd conclusion, when violence breaks out before him and he does nothing to stop it. Once Gallio dismisses the Jewish accusers, some people seize Sosthenes, a synagogue official, and beat him in public. The syntax suggests that it is the Jewish accusers who assault Sosthenes. Why? Perhaps he, like Crispus before him, also counts himself among Jesus's followers, even though nothing in Acts indicates this. More likely, the group of Jews beats one of its own leaders. Maybe they are enraged at having been snubbed and humiliated by Gallio, and they blame the synagogue official for making such an unconvincing case to the governor.

The incident is troubling; it presents yet another instance of violence wrapped in burlesque, where someone receives what are presumably just deserts for opposing God's representatives or perverting the gospel's reputation, as with Simon the magician in Acts 8 and a group of exorcists in Acts 19. It raises disturbing questions when Jesus promises to protect Paul in Corinth but poor Sosthenes is left on his own.

At the end of the story, the accusers look disorganized, desperate, and violent—neither the first nor the last time Acts portrays the gospel's opponents in such unflattering light. Equally alarming, the Roman governor comes across as either an idiot or a bully, not a savvy defender of Paul and emerging Christianity, but contemptuous toward Jewish concerns and tacitly endorsing mob violence in his midst. Gallio shows himself not so concerned about crime or villainy after all, for he's fully willing to let his Jewish subjects tear one another apart. As the leading representative of Roman authority in the region, Gallio's disdain paints Rome as ignorant about Christianity's claims and their relevance for the wider gentile population. If he merely has scorn for Jews, that may extend to the God that they (and the church) serve. Granted, Paul's message would likely sound totally strange to him. But since he will not even hear it, we cannot know.

In Gallio, we see just how foreign and uninteresting the God of Israel and the gospel of Christ appear to a Roman authority with significant power and responsibility.

Paul's Jewish identity never fades from view in this scene. His change in ministry strategy does not erase it; it only calls attention to it. Immediately after this scene ends, in 18:18, Paul fulfills a vow, indicating his ongoing commitment to a tradition in Jewish piety. Paul's accusers see him as a Jew, as does Gallio. Jewish identity contributes to the tensions in this episode.

The brief hearing and then the attack on Sosthenes right under the governor's dismissive nose remind readers of the social and physical hostilities that Jews sometimes had to endure in certain parts of the Roman Empire. Within the bright and diverse cultural mosaic that was Corinth, Paul and his associates come across as disadvantaged people who should not expect to enjoy prominence or even general regard. The passage begins, remember, by introducing Aquila and Priscilla as refugees, displaced from their home by the Roman emperor because they—or at least Aquila—were Jewish. Even their trade in Corinth carries a hint of diminished status: tentmaking was not a particularly respectable occupation among the artisan class. Was this the work they wanted to do, or the only work they could find as newcomers with little prestige in this multicultural city?

All the Jews in this passage are people whom the local power brokers could easily overlook, and it seems Gallio is the type prone to do exactly that. Fortunately for Paul, he falls on the fortunate side of Gallio's lack of interest and avoids real legal and physical jeopardy in Corinth. It won't always go this well for Paul in the upcoming chapters of Acts. Governors come across as a temperamental bunch; their capriciousness can strike in any direction, often increasing instead of reducing antagonisms.

Clearly Gallio's lack of concern for a beaten man differs from Jesus's assurance that no one in Corinth will harm Paul. An even sharper contrast exists, however, between Jesus's keen knowledge about the "many in this city" who are his people and the governor's disregard for Paul's gospel and the controversy it generates within the local Jewish community. Jesus perceives the potential for the church to take root in this city. Gallio can't make the connection; either he does not recognize the potential or he does not care.

As Acts sees it, the gospel is strange. Sometimes the Christian message and its potential to upend the status quo go unnoticed by the bigwigs in society. Sometimes, as we will see throughout Acts 22–28, the powerful pay attention.

At the same time, gaining their attention will change hardly anything. "Success" in Acts does not depend on gaining respectability. Neither is avoiding respectability a sign of true faithfulness. So much about Christianity in the modern Western world has been about pursuing and maintaining respectability, in cultural and ethical terms. Even though a few New Testament writings place a high value on Christians' efforts to gain respectability in their neighbors' eyes, Acts is much less concerned about this. The portrayal of Gallio in Acts indicates such pursuits are hardly worth the effort anyway. Whether encountering violent hostility in Philippi, amused curiosity in Athens, disdainful apathy in Corinth, or an economically motivated protest in Ephesus (coming in Acts 19), those who bear authentic witness to Jesus in Acts urge readers to heed the words that the Lord speaks to encourage Paul: "Speak and do not be silent."

Paul will keep doing exactly that. He listens, and he sees. Gallio does not. As a result, the governor can guarantee no one's safety. He makes us recall why God's salvation is needful in the first place.

Acts 18:24–19:20

There's Power in the Name

So the word of the Lord grew mightily and prevailed.
(Acts 19:20)

I used to think "taking the Lord's name in vain" was about things
I shouldn't blurt out when I stub my toe in a dark room. Instead, it
has more to do with taking God's power lightly or presuming I can
manipulate that power. This is important to consider when we read
about the Christian communities in Acts as communities equipped
and united by Jesus's "name."

Paul and his companions arrive in Ephesus in 18:19. A coastal city
located on the western edge of present-day Turkey and rich in natural
resources, Ephesus was a major commercial hub. About a quarter mil-
lion people lived there. In the Roman Empire during the first century,
only Rome, Alexandria, and Syrian Antioch could boast of larger
populations. Acts indicates Paul and other Christian missionaries
made Ephesus a center of their operations, and Paul maintains a rather
visible presence there. He devotes himself to regular public speaking
in both the local Jewish synagogue and a place, otherwise unknown
from ancient sources, called the school of Tyrannus—apparently
a guildhall or some other form of public meeting space owned by,
associated with, or used by a man named Tyrannus.

Although Paul spends over two years working in Ephesus, Acts describes next to nothing about the establishment, growth, and organization of a church there. Obviously Paul and his friends do establish or discover an Ephesian church, or perhaps multiple small Christian communities, because later in Acts he meets with its leaders (20:17–38). The narrative prefers to focus readers' attention on episodes about the equipping and the triumph of this church. It's an additional reminder about the overall purpose of the book of Acts: less interested in mapping the process of how the church grew or describing how it rightly functions, more interested in declaring that God guides the church as it spreads the gospel into various settings, often disrupting business as usual in the process.

The first half of this passage shows people building up and instructing others in the community of faith; the second half addresses the church's potential to confront and obstruct evil.

Just prior to settling down in Ephesus, Paul takes a briefly described detour much farther to the east, "strengthening all the disciples" in different regions of Asia Minor. His itinerary reiterates that his ministry involves more than evangelizing in public and founding new churches; he also labors to sustain Christian communities. This endeavor sets the tone for two scenes about disciples receiving instruction in Ephesus. Both scenes reaffirm the importance of training and sustaining churches.

First, a passionate and eloquent teacher named Apollos arrives. Like Paul, he's a Jew who follows Jesus Christ. Still, Apollos has a deficiency: his knowledge, although accurate, remains incomplete because he knows "only the baptism of John." Does this make him merely unaware of the practice of baptism in Jesus's name, or could he be more broadly ignorant of Jesus's ministry and what set it apart from John the Baptizer's preaching about repentance? In either case, Apollos needs to learn.

Paul's companions, Priscilla and Aquila, the couple he met previously in Corinth (18:2), take up the task. Without publicly humiliating or denouncing him, they take Apollos aside and instruct him. Because Acts, defying convention, lists Priscilla's name before her husband's, we can assume she takes the lead in this work. It's a subtle reminder about public Christian leadership in Acts: it rightly belongs to women and men, like Peter said back on Pentecost. As a result of this cooperative conversation, Apollos himself becomes a more effective minister, able to assist other believers he encounters after leaving Ephesus.

A similar scene follows at the beginning of Acts 19. Paul encounters about a dozen "disciples" in Ephesus who have no knowledge of either the Holy Spirit or a Christian baptism in the name of the Lord Jesus. Perhaps these people had participated in John the Baptizer's ministry but never heard about Jesus or understood his connections to John. More likely, they resemble Apollos as followers of Jesus who need more comprehensive instruction.

These disciples also resemble the Samaritan converts in Acts 8:14–17, who did not receive the Holy Spirit until Peter and John laid their hands on them. As in that scene, when Paul puts his hands on the people in Ephesus, he expresses their integration as members of the wider Christian community.

From these two scenes of correction and teaching, the image emerges of a church that by no means has everything perfectly organized. People need instruction; they need formal recognition and integration into the broader community; the church needs all of its resources, and all of its people, for its mutual work to succeed. If the church will articulate God's salvation adequately, everyone must fully belong.

These scenes about the upbuilding of the church come across as rather ordinary in light of the usual dramatic fare Acts serves us. The fireworks return in 19:11, but the ordinary church maintenance that comes first gives us clearer insight into the wilder episodes to come. Keep in mind the cooperative, communal aspects of 18:24–19:7 and how they lift up the importance of relationships, communication, and openness to others.

Acts doesn't make much of miracles Paul performs, but 19:11–12 brings a notable exception, with its mention of healing handkerchiefs and other things that appear to convey power from Paul's body to where it is needed. This is another case—like Paul's healing of a man unable to walk in Acts 14—in which the narrative urges us to see Paul in connection to Peter (5:15), and both of them in connection to Jesus (Luke 8:44). All three of these men exhibit astonishing power, but Acts refuses to let us forget the source of the wonders. Paul doesn't perform the miracles; according to 19:11, God does.

The seven sons of Sceva appear to miss that detail. They act as if human beings can manipulate God's power on their terms. According to Acts, the traveling exorcists invoke "the name of the Lord Jesus" to gain power over evil spirits.

These men operate as comic foils in the story. Records from antiquity never mention any Sceva in a catalog of Jewish high priests, and the name appears to be of Latin and not Hebrew or Greek origin anyway. These details imply mischief or falsehood. Are the seven charlatans? While plenty of ancient sources refer to people who performed exorcisms (including Luke 9:49–50; 11:19), these brothers look like scammers. They try to ride on the coattails of Jesus's and Paul's renown.

Perhaps we can give them credit for recognizing the power associated with the name of Jesus (see also 4:10, 30; 16:18; 19:5–6), but not for their intention to use it as a talisman. Still, they are not entirely unusual. Documents containing magical formulas have survived from antiquity; some of them invoke names of deities, including names of God used in the Old Testament and even Jesus's name. To use a "name" like this, or to assert an action done in the power of another's "name," is to identify with the one who possesses that name, to act as a representative. It is to claim the authority of that person—or that deity—in an action.

Of course, the exorcism goes awry and produces a comical scene, leaving once proud, now naked, exorcists running for their lives. (Not so funny are the violence and humiliation suffered by the exorcists and the ongoing suffering of the possessed man. But the account aspires to comic-book-quality humor, not serious ethical reflection on all the consequences.) Jesus's name will not be manipulated. Simon the magician learned a similar lesson in Acts 8.

As a result of the spectacle, the name of Jesus returns to its proper function: the object of people's praise (19:17). New converts to the

Christian faith, acknowledging the power of Jesus's name and its incommensurability with magical arts that seek to harness spiritual power for personal gain, publicly repudiate their past practices and make a radical break. They burn their magical writings, which may themselves have been associated with the cultural climate in Ephesus, for the city was known for producing such documents.

Many kinds of magic were practiced and widely assumed to wield real power in the ancient world, so it is difficult to generalize about exactly what these magicians did previously. Nevertheless, magical practices commonly involved barbaric treatment of people and animals. Rituals and concoctions inflicted people with acute suffering. Some magical acts aimed to manipulate the spiritual world to gain control over an unwitting person. As we saw with Simon the magician in Acts 8, the narrative views magic very critically and understands it to have strong associations with exploitation and greed. The value of the destroyed books confirms this association. Acts does not identify the specific coinage in question, but fifty thousand of any kind of silver coin would equal a vast sum. New converts join the Christian community willing to suffer economic loss as they separate themselves from their previous abusive practices.

Taken on their own, the stories of the impudent exorcists and the book-burning magicians warn against the misuse of spiritual power and perhaps show the gospel's superiority over other spiritual forces. As with other parts of the New Testament, they affirm the reality of evil and the ways humanity falls victim to it even as we try to resist its hold over us. A whole book would be required to answer questions about whether demons or unclean spirits really exist, how we should characterize evil, and why some cultures embrace magic and other means of controlling human experience; this exploration cannot go into the finer details.

Note, however, that through its references to demonic beings, the New Testament understands evil as a real, destructive part of human experience. And, as we know all too well, people find themselves oppressed by many things, whether we understand those in spiritual, psychological, medical, or sociological terms. These oppressive conditions and forces frequently confound our ability to control them; they remind us of the many ways in which our problems exceed our ability to provide solutions. To assert the name of Jesus as a way to find shelter from evil is to move to a higher level; the gospel claims this name's reach is cosmic and total. But the gravity of evil, well known in human experience, issues us stern warnings against cavalierly claiming Jesus's ability to nullify it or provide us with simple or instant relief. The corrosive power of hate, unbreakable cycles of injustice and degradation, people's gratuitous manipulation of others for their own benefit—these and other forms of evil are enormous issues. Any talk about Jesus's name must take this seriously.

We must also view the passage's references to exorcisms and spiritual powers in connection to the material that precedes them. Recall Priscilla, Aquila, and Paul as they contribute to the well-being of the Christian community so its members might experience the fullness of the gospel's promises and engage in ministry to benefit others. The cooperative, interdependent nature of that community and the ministry it conducts says something about what "the name of the Lord Jesus" is really all about. It's the name and the power at the heart of the baptism uniting all members of this community to one another.

We can consider Sceva's sons reprehensible and foolish, not because they are self-aggrandizing, but because their spectacle stands in such contrast to the snapshots Acts offers to display the church in action just prior to the point where the brothers enter the story. Maybe the evil spirit that castigates the seven of them sees the whole picture. When this spirit says it knows Jesus and Paul but cannot recognize the exorcists, we realize how out of step their pretense really appears in contrast to the true gospel—how contrary it is to true expressions of the power of Jesus's name. I imagine the evil spirit's rebuke following a logic like this:

> How dare you presume to know what you're talking about? The power that comes from Jesus means more than brandishing a word. It's not about blithely claiming someone else's authority over truly destructive powers and moving on to your next challenge or payday. It's not even about a spiritual leader like Paul laying his hands on people and welcoming them into full fellowship with himself and his Lord.

No, I've seen the power that Jesus gives, and I know what the consequences are for evil. That power has nothing to do with using the right words in the right settings to effect the desired outcome. I saw it earlier in Ephesus: it's a power you see when people work together—to care for each other and to instruct one another in the truth. It's when dynamic public speakers humbly receive correction from women and men they hardly know. It's when people travel to strange lands to offer support, encouragement, and instruction to disciples over there. It's when someone like Paul finds common ground with others and works toward mutual understanding, eagerly willing to include and welcome those who formerly were outsiders. It's when people quit exploiting their neighbors' vulnerabilities. When all this happens, they *refuse* to lord their knowledge or power over others but join with them in authentic solidarity to be means by which God's purposes might come to fruition. That's the only kind of power that drives out evil.

Your selfish, opportunistic attempts to appropriate the power that truly stems from Jesus and the salvation he brings make you just as guilty of violence and exploitation as I am.

Acts 19:21–41

Far-Reaching Disruptions

> This Paul has persuaded and drawn away a considerable
> number of people. (Acts 19:26)

Overcoming the local exorcists and magicians in Ephesus previously, in Acts 19, was one thing. Now the tension mounts for Paul and others. The gospel they speak and embody gets people talking about topics that can make for uncomfortable and disorderly conversations: politics, religion, economics.

Earlier, when consulting narrative road maps before exploring both Acts 13:1–4 and Acts 16:9–40, I noted that most of Acts 13–19 describes Paul's travels to preach the gospel throughout cites in Greece, Macedonia, and Asia Minor (modern Turkey). Also, most of these scenes illustrate the disruptive nature of the Christian gospel as its claims and communities confront the various cultural values represented by those urban centers. This trajectory clearly continues in the second half of Acts 19, as Paul and his associates remain in Ephesus and encounter resistance.

Before the trouble erupts, however, the beginning of this passage indicates a new phase is about to begin in Paul's story. We read, "Paul resolved in the Spirit to go through Macedonia and Achaia, and then to go on to Jerusalem. He said, 'After I have gone there, I must also see Rome.'" This statement builds an additional parallel between Paul

143

and Jesus, who, in the middle of his public ministry in Luke 9:51, "set his face to go to Jerusalem." Jerusalem would mean Jesus's rejection and death, and for Paul it will mean arrest. This arrest will finally result in death, after Paul gets to Rome. (Acts does not narrate Paul's execution, but some verses clearly anticipate it, especially a poignant farewell he gives to the leaders of the Ephesian church in 20:17–38.)

Paul does not resolve to go to these places because he has a death wish or because he himself crafts his career to mimic Jesus's; the resolution is entirely God's. The Spirit somehow discloses Paul's future to him. His work among the peoples of the northeastern Mediterranean will cease, but his role as Jesus's witness will not. Paul will find new audiences in new venues. First, however, one more scene of high adventure awaits in Ephesus.

Ancient Ephesus enjoyed renown for several reasons, including its relationship to the goddess Artemis (who was usually considered equivalent to Diana in Latin-based Roman mythology). Goddess of the hunt, of childbirth, and of death as well as a healer of women, Artemis also enjoyed very high regard from people outside Ephesus, but the Ephesians' devotion to her was well established. Artemis worship had been central to religious and civic life in Ephesus for over ten centuries leading up to the advent of Christianity. No wonder, then, that a legend circulated about a statue of Artemis in Ephesus, that it had fallen from heaven (19:35). The local temple of Artemis made the list of the Seven Wonders of the ancient world. It also functioned as a bank, a well-funded one. Upon hearing the name Ephesus, people in the Roman Empire would think of Artemis, and vice versa. She and the religious system associated with her provided a core piece of the city's corporate identity and financial vitality.

When a reference is made, in 19:27, to Artemis's majesty and its ability to bring "all Asia and the world to worship her" in Ephesus, the exaggeration is not as far-fetched as it might sound. She is no regional deity. Neither is the God Paul talks about.

Paul's prolonged ministry in Ephesus, lasting over two years (19:8–10), proves successful enough to attract the attention of those who do not join the church. These people occupy the narrative stage in this passage; neither Paul nor any of his associates speak. The result is a look at the gospel and its effects through the eyes of outsiders, members of a larger society in which the gospel is beginning to take root. One group of these people has a particularly large stake in the city's attachments to Artemis. A silversmith named Demetrius recognizes that converts to Christianity abandon polytheism and that Paul's preaching includes criticism of those who assume a deity can be present in a statue or temple (recall Paul's oratory to the Areopagite Council in Athens, back in Acts 17). These developments threaten the silversmith business, driving down demand for miniature statues of the goddess and replicas of her majestic temple.

Demetrius may be jumping the gun, or perhaps he uses the specter of economic hardship to mask other reasons for opposing the gospel. A tremendous number of converts to Christ would have been necessary to pose serious harm to the silversmiths' business among both locals and pilgrims, and no evidence exists to indicate the original Christian community in Ephesus was so large. But it is too simple to accuse Demetrius of only base greed or cultural arrogance. Through clear insight or just dumb, ironic luck, he seems to have put his finger on a dynamic that Acts accentuates for readers: the gospel has repercussions for how people spend their money and construct their identities. While Demetrius's tactics—rousing a crowd into an angry, slightly alarmist, and perhaps volatile demonstration—may be contemptible, he understands that the Christian church's propagation in Ephesus will not leave the wider culture unaltered. Demetrius fears for his bank account but also for what might gradually diminish the proud reputation of his city.

Demetrius quickly drops out of the narrative's spotlight. Did things get out of control, beyond his intentions? At the end of the scene he will be remembered as a principal instigator. In any case, the episode quickly turns frightening. The city falls into confusion. Two of Paul's partners are dragged into a tumult. High-ranking officials caution Paul about the danger. The narrator refers to many people in the commotion who don't even know what's going on. A Jew named Alexander gets shouted down before we can learn who he is, who urges him to come forward, or what he intends to tell the crowd. The mob chants a slogan in unison for two hours straight.

The narrator does not mention the size of the demonstration, but it occurs in a large venue; remains of the theater in Ephesus reveal it could hold over twenty-four thousand people. If this incident took place today, hundreds of security personnel or police officers in riot gear would gather nearby weighing the idea of dispersing the crowd before real mayhem detonated. What begins as ostensible concern over Demetrius's business now includes, warranted or not, widespread agitation about Ephesus's civic pride, international reputation, and financial stability.

At this point, given the flair for the dramatic in Acts, we might expect Paul to enter the theater to refute the crowd's claims or suffer its wrath. But a simple resolution to the crisis comes instead through the sober admonitions of the town clerk (a significant office in the city's administration). This man says, in essence, "Relax. We all know everyone loves Ephesus for good reasons." The clerk suggests Artemis can fend for herself, yet he doesn't address the precipitating question of whether the Christian faith might progressively turn people away from Artemis and the commerce rooted in her popularity. He simply notes that the men in the crosshairs of the crowd's immediate wrath, Gaius and Aristarchus, do not actively oppose Artemis or explicitly threaten the glories of her temple and her fair city. If people disagree, he says, if their complaints have real substance, they should make use of the legal avenues available to them: "The courts are open."

The clerk's closing words may prove the most effective: he worries aloud about the possibility of being prosecuted for rioting, a transgression Roman officials usually took very seriously and were compelled to punish. The crowd lowers its fists and walks away. The demonstration ends quietly.

Wisely, Paul leaves town right away, in the very next verse (20:1). Perhaps he recognizes this conflict will soon flare up again because the protestors were onto something. Demetrius's core concern remains valid: the Ephesian religious industrial complex cannot expect to remain completely unaffected as long as some Ephesians embrace the gospel and continue to tell their neighbors about it.

The way Acts tells the story, no opportunity arises to weigh Demetrius's complaints against the town clerk's speech. Obviously the clerk's words would not negate the silversmiths' chief concerns about the future of their livelihoods. The clerk's greatest worry appears to be the manner of the protest—its size and volatility. Perhaps he underestimates a risk that Demetrius and company overestimate. What does the rest of the city think? We can't be sure, which only escalates the drama.

Demetrius perceives in the gospel a threat to his pocketbook; this much is obvious. But he also sees a threat to the Ephesians' civil religion and, by extension, to their basic cultural identity. Ancient Greek and Roman polytheism had room for multiple deities and mutual respect among various forms of religious devotion, but to Demetrius this new Christian faith, with its one true God and its clear, exclusive focus on Jesus, appears intent on playing by different rules.

The disturbance in Ephesus raises questions about Christianity's ability to coexist with other religions. Acts certainly shows no interest in affirming other religions' validity as commendable options alongside the Christian faith, even though it does acknowledge (in Paul's words to the Lystrans and Athenians in Acts 14 and 17) ways in which people might be drawn to God apart from preaching about Jesus. But Acts also does not operate with any awareness of the principles of pluralism and tolerance that make modern Western democracy possible. The latter half of Acts 19 does not necessarily advance a desire for Christianity to obliterate all other forms of religious expression, but it does make us wonder whether Acts has anything constructive to say to challenges we face concerning coexistence and constructive dialogue across religious lines. The status of Christianity in the Western world today commends more humility and openness than perhaps Acts is willing to recognize or grant in its original ancient circumstances. Modern Christians have, out of necessity and reason, taken different approaches to these issues.

At the same time, this passage also puts before us questions about civil religion and the ways in which religious identity gets made to serve a people's economic and political interests for good or (too often) for ill. American and other democratic cultures tout the values of separating church and state, and rightly so. But this separation speaks to a legal distinction; it does not expect us to isolate our religious,

political, and cultural identities in separate, self-contained boxes, as
if this were even possible. So much of American Christianity reflects
American cultural values, and vice versa. We can never completely
undo this. Yet shining a light onto it and becoming more aware of
the complexity of our agendas and morals might make us better able
to hear the voice of God. To do so, we must distinguish this voice
from the noise generated by our tendencies to confuse nationalism
with discipleship.

What has to go when the gospel takes hold in a culture or in a
person? Are there forms of patriotism or core economic assumptions
that must take a backseat—or be booted out of the car—for a person
to realize her true and full Christian identity?

How do God's intentions, discovered in the imperatives and values expressed by the gospel of Jesus Christ, call into question basic
assumptions we have about our personal rights and our economic
practices? If people start taking the gospel too seriously, will we as
individuals and nations have to start doing different things with our
money? Compassion to the neighbor can add up, after all. It gets
expensive. Are there elements of our society's consumerism mentality that have to go? How disruptive can we afford to let this gospel
become?

When God's salvation comes to town, choices and changes like
these have the potential to make Christians appear strange—perhaps
even dangerous. Acts recognizes this. The book comes from a time
in history when refusal to honor a local god was more than a religious preference; it was potentially a seditious act. When a famine
or drought struck, how would the wider society view the group of
people who had stopped worshiping the deity who was expected to
grant a bountiful harvest? Or, when a modern nation-state expects
its population to pursue self-interest or self-defense as primary and
unassailable values, how will it view the members of its population
who choose instead to love the vulnerable in their midst and the
strangers at their borders as much as they love themselves?

The gospel presented in Acts continues to disturb what we thought
was merely business as usual. This happens not only for every Saint

Francis, Martin Luther King Jr., or Mother Teresa who comes along; our more ordinary and incremental opportunities to practice forgiveness, justice, and generosity have consequences too. Add up all these intrusions into the status quo, and things can get pretty disorderly in a hurry.

Road Map

The Witness Goes to Rome

After the excitement in Ephesus dissipates at the end Acts 19—or, as it says in 20:1, "after the uproar had ceased"—Paul begins a meandering journey back to Jerusalem. The next chapter in our exploration, which explores 21:1–6, comments on details of this trip because they help inform the mood in that passage. Generally speaking, Acts 20 is a transitional part of the narrative. Paul goes to Jerusalem confident that suffering awaits him there. He encourages other Christians as he makes the trek. Our anticipation swells as we follow along on this journey, waiting to learn what will happen.

Not long after his arrival in Jerusalem in 21:17, a group of antagonists seizes Paul, and he winds up in Roman custody. He's never released. From his arrest onward, through Acts 28, the entire last quarter of Acts reads like a different kind of story—one packed with political intrigue, legal maneuvering, a couple of long speeches, and a lot of waiting.

It's not that Acts transforms into a legal drama; instead, it remains a drama about God's involvement in the life of Jesus's followers even as one of those followers, Paul, transitions into a different kind of cultural environment. This environment is a legal one, but the success or failure of navigating it depends little on his ability to prove whether he has broken any laws. The legal world of a far-flung first-century province like Judea was not exactly orderly and principled, as exemplified in the judicial theatrics of Jesus's prosecution in the four Gospels. Paul's ability to stay out of mortal danger depends on whether he can persuade the right people that he poses no threat either to social order or to some people's understandings of Jewish values. A question drives much of the action: Can Paul do this while still holding true to his identity as a witness to Jesus Christ?

Acts never lets us forget that Paul remains Jesus's witness. He speaks about the gospel to the most powerful people in the area: a high priest and his council, Roman military leaders, provincial governors, and a client king. The speeches he gives allow him to address the controversy he causes within some Jewish groups as well as the concerns Roman officials have about what makes him such a polarizing figure among his people.

The final chapters of our investigation of Acts summarize much of the description of Paul's legal travails. As you read through this material, notice how much influence Paul exercises over his circumstances. He's a prisoner, so his influence stays confined within strict boundaries, but nevertheless Acts focuses more on his freedoms than his limitations. This focus makes a statement: not one about the power of positive thinking or about clouds having silver linings but a statement about Paul's ability to continue bearing witness to Jesus despite the restrictions imposed by Roman authority. Paul's case does not seem like the kind of thing that would have attracted so much attention from so many Roman officials. But in this story, it does. With its emphatic portrait of Paul, Acts makes assertions about the gospel's persistent influence and God's determination to have the good news of salvation find a hearing everywhere, even in those places where other authorities seem to wield tight control over who gets to do what.

The word of God, Acts declares, will persist even in the face of unrelenting efforts to keep it restrained.

Acts 21:1–6

Spirit-Led Disagreement

Through the Spirit they told Paul not to go on to Jerusalem. (Acts 21:4)

From the *news of the obvious* department: Christians with good intentions have been known to disagree with one another.

Anyone who doubts this needs to spend more time in church. People who denounce disagreement as an indication of dysfunctional fellowship, or who consider conflict incongruous with Christian living, need to spend more time reading the Bible. We in the church get caught pining for a golden age in church history that never existed whenever we conjure false memories of *everyone* in a Christian community getting along in perfect agreement. The New Testament hardly gives evidence for such an age existing in the earliest generations of the church.

Even Acts, in its most idealistic moments, cannot muster more than a few sentences about communal harmony. As we have seen, the corporate life of the community of believers in Jerusalem looks wonderful in the final verses of Acts 2 and 4. But these descriptions vanish from the narrative like vapor in a breeze, and Acts never again expresses much interest in the possibility or necessity of returning to the good old days. Recall Ananias and Sapphira (Acts 5) and the complaints about the slighting of Hellenist widows (Acts 6). Pointed disagreement over how to conduct the Lord's work led even stalwart Paul and Barnabas to dissolve their close-knit partnership in 15:36–41. Readers can only hope the two evangelists remained friends, for their separation marks Barnabas's final mention in Acts. He, like many others in the book, simply disappears from sight.

Rarely does Acts fret about disagreements within the church. Sometimes, as we have seen in Acts 10–11 and Acts 15, internal controversies provide a stimulus for believers to discern together where they see God initiating new directions to follow. Differences of theological opinion in those passages do not stem from spiritual laziness or unfaithfulness; they create occasions for people to turn to God and collectively reexamine their theological assumptions in light of other evidence they have encountered. In these instances, Acts describes the Holy Spirit guiding people through surprising discoveries about God's intentions.

Given the ways Acts usually celebrates the Spirit's guidance and people's efforts to discern the Spirit, we might be tempted to conclude that the book papers over the potential for well-meaning Christians to *persist* in disagreement. Because of 21:1–6, however, such a conclusion would be a mistake. In this scene, Acts acknowledges struggles can come even with resolute efforts to discern God's presence and leading. In fact, in this instance God's own Spirit appears to be the source or instigator of sharp disagreement. The Spirit seems uninterested in engineering an easy solution for people who cannot reconcile differing opinions about which path to follow.

At the beginning of Acts 21, Paul and his co-travelers arrive in Tyre, a major city on the Mediterranean Sea's eastern shore, where they spend a week with the local Christians. This stopover comes near the end of Paul's final journey as a free man. He is traveling southward, returning to Jerusalem according to the plan he announced while living in Ephesus, in Acts 19:21. At that time, we learned: "Paul resolved in the Spirit to go through Macedonia and Achaia, and then to go on to Jerusalem. He said, 'After I have gone there, I must also see Rome.'"

As he followed his itinerary from Ephesus to Tyre in Acts 20, the narrative indicates he continued with a clear confidence in the

Spirit's guidance. En route he paused to speak hopefully and tenderly to a group of church leaders, telling them, "And now, as a captive to the Spirit, I am on my way to Jerusalem, not knowing what will happen to me there, except that the Holy Spirit testifies to me in every city that imprisonment and persecutions are waiting for me. But I do not count my life of any value to myself, if only I may finish my course and the ministry that I received from the Lord Jesus, to testify to the good news of God's grace" (20:22–24). The rest of Paul's speech and visit in 20:17–38, along with the escalating animus toward him throughout the controversies recounted in Acts 16–19, contribute to an ominous sense of suffering and death hovering over his journey. His determination persisted, nevertheless, countering the dire mood. When he raised a young man named Eutychus from the dead in 20:7–12, the life-affirming character of his ministry glowed brighter.

Paul moves toward Jerusalem, then, not out of a suicidal impulse or a dread-laden resignation but in response to his clear convictions about what God's Spirit has put before him.

The rapid-pace narration of Paul's journey along an established trade route at the start of Acts 21 slows just enough when he reaches Tyre to reveal that obeying the Spirit is not as simple as the story thus far might have suggested. The briefly narrated events in Tyre underscore the difficulty of being responsive to God even as they lift up the importance of mutual concern among Jesus's followers.

As Paul and his colleagues enjoy hospitality from fellow believers in Tyre, the Tyrians entreat him—through the Spirit—not to continue to Jerusalem. Those three words *through the Spirit* in 21:4 should catch our attention. They suggest more than just heartfelt sincerity from Paul's hosts. Somehow, the Holy Spirit figures in their appeal.

What does this mean? Acts leaves us to speculate. Has the Holy Spirit fashioned a new plan for Paul and so no longer intends for him to return to Jerusalem? Presumably Paul does not believe this, since he resumes his journey at the scene's conclusion.

Is the Spirit playing games with Paul, or testing his resolve? This too is unlikely, for it would suggest a completely new and unexpected *modus operandi* for the Holy Spirit in Luke and Acts. Also, nothing in the narration points to a test.

Have the disciples in Tyre misinterpreted the voice of the Spirit, or could they willfully attempt to deceive Paul? Nothing in the story supports these possibilities either. We would expect, as we have seen elsewhere in Acts, withering denunciation of people who dare to exploit the Spirit for their own ends. Furthermore, the rest of this scene characterizes these people as earnest and warmhearted.

Have they seen the writing on the wall, or have they heard from Paul about the violent future he expects in Jerusalem, and simply assumed God could never allow such an end to befall someone as valuable or faithful as Paul? Although despair at the prospect of losing Paul seems to be present in a later passage, when Paul visits Christians farther south, in Caesarea (21:8–16), nothing about the events in Tyre intimates that the believers there reason in the same way.

So, what's going on? It appears that the Tyrians' appeal to Paul "through the Spirit" indicates they understand the Holy Spirit as desiring a certain course of action for Paul—avoiding Jerusalem. Their appeal to the Spirit could be as basic as if they say to him, "Think about what the Holy Spirit would have you do in this situation!" and he replies, "I have." But their language comes across stronger than that: they make their plea as something authorized by the Spirit (see similar language in 1:2; 11:28). This means different Christians are interpreting the will of the Spirit in contradictory ways. Paul senses the Spirit leading one way; the Tyrians, another way. Whether Paul actively debates them, we do not know. Clearly, however, he is not finally convinced by their convictions. He follows his own. The two parties simply disagree.

Many Christians suffer no shock at reading about different believers interpreting the prompting of the Holy Spirit in divergent ways. But this passage's brevity and subtlety discourage us from simply writing off the Tyrians as wrong, misguided, or naive. Their appeal "through the Spirit" raises the possibility that different groups reach differing conclusions, both derived from attending faithfully to the Spirit's presence. This makes for a unique scene in Acts, given the book's usual confidence in the effectiveness of the Spirit's guidance. The exceptional character of this passage issues a quiet caution to us against overplaying our assumptions about God as predictable or easy to figure out if we just listen really carefully together.

The opacity of this scene's reference to the Spirit nevertheless joins other passages in Acts to issue a clear point: the Holy Spirit is radically free and often difficult to grasp. Keeping pace with God's Spirit requires people to engage in theological discernment—with those who agree with them concerning the content of the Spirit's leadings and with those who disagree. No wonder Paul stays in Tyre for seven days. We can only imagine the lively conversations he shares with the Tyrians and the stress they experience.

Christians often look to the Holy Spirit for the means and inspiration to reconcile differences. What if the Spirit also *contributes* to conflict or to differing opinions among believers? This passage holds out the possibility that opposing convictions can originate from the Spirit's influence. At first blush, such an assertion may pose serious problems. If the Spirit leads like this, how can God possibly expect to be known among Christians? How can we ever hope for those who observe Christian communities from the outside to see evidence of the Spirit among us? Can the Spirit even be recognized in the midst of division?

The rest of the scene in Tyre offers answers. If the expression *through the Spirit* only ambiguously locates the *source* of differing opinions between Paul and his friends in the Spirit, the narrative makes a much stronger statement about the Spirit's role within Christian community through the *outcome* of this disagreement. Notice again the passage's ending, for it, too, expresses the Spirit's presence: "When our days there were ended, we left and proceeded on our journey; and all of them, with wives and children, escorted us outside the city. There we knelt down on the beach and prayed and said farewell to one another. Then we went on board the ship, and they returned home."

The beach provides a fitting setting. There, where water divides from land, where a traveler starts a journey, the Tyrians send Paul and his companions on their way. The Spirit is present there too—not just on the sand but also in the sympathy. Encountering God's Spirit isn't just about figuring out what decision to make; it's also about experiencing the joy and the distress that come from being committed to other people, even people with whom we might disagree.

Not only is God present in the pain we feel when discord arises; the Spirit experiences it as well. The Tyrians' appeal to Paul "in the Spirit" likely indicates that they are not alone in their deep concern about what awaits Paul in Jerusalem. We can presume the Spirit grieves for adversities Paul will endure there and beyond.

Perhaps most remarkable about this story is not its suggestion of the Holy Spirit giving two contrary messages to two different groups. Rather, a community of people, experiencing fundamental disagreement over how to respond faithfully to the Holy Spirit, stays in communion. Neither Paul nor the Tyrians give up on the other. How can the Spirit be visible amid Christians holding opposed spiritual convictions? In this way: the Spirit preserves a bond of unity, dramatically enacted when Paul and the believers of Tyre—all the men, women, and children—pray together on the beach. The scene closes not with a quarrel but with shared commitment. It's a good thing the children were brought along to the beach to learn what unity looks like. This closing image presents us with the Spirit's deep involvement in a potentially painful farewell, which should prevent us from dismissing the scene as mawkish. God's Spirit might disrupt the prospects of Christians finding comfort in a total unanimity of opinion, but this does not mean God is uninterested in preserving unity among believers. Neither is God unwilling to suffer among them.

Paul leaves Tyre for Jerusalem, choosing to follow the leading of the Holy Spirit as he has discerned it. The church of Tyre sends him on his way, even though Paul in the end does not heed their appeal. In solidarity outside the city walls, everyone participates in initiating the next leg of Paul's travels. No schism. No threats. No denunciations. All of them pray to the same God, then the two groups return to their respective business, each seeking to be faithful to what they believe God has called them to do next.

Acts 22:30–23:11

How to Be a Hero

That night the Lord stood near him and said, "Keep up your courage!" (Acts 23:11)

No wonder in Acts 21 the disciples in Tyre didn't want Paul to go to Jerusalem. It's hard to let go of our heroes.

Paul's return to Jerusalem, the city where he launched his persecution of Christians so long ago (8:1–3; 9:1–2), proceeds pretty much according to expectations. Paul, informed by the Holy Spirit, prepares for hardship (20:22–24). A future-seeing prophet in Caesarea predicts Paul's arrest (21:10–11). Sure enough, less than a dozen verses after his arrival (21:17), Paul finds himself seized by an enraged crowd (21:27) in the temple complex. Before this group can finish beating him to death, the Roman military swoops in to snatch Paul and ferry him to a safe place above the crowd (21:30–34). He remains in custody of one kind or another from this point until the end of Acts.

The earliest hours of his detention unfold like an action film, with a clear hero, obvious villains, and others trying to make sense of the chaos. Perilous scenarios end with clever, last-second getaways that nevertheless lead back into the teeth of danger. The enraged crowd at the temple still wants to kill Paul, believing, apparently without warrant, that he has repudiated Judaism and illegally brought gentiles into the temple. The Romans mistake him for an Egyptian revolutionary.

Paul's attempt to explain himself to the seething assembly further
enrages them. The Roman soldiers, unable or unwilling to figure out
what is at the root of the crowd's violent opposition, decide torture
will extract the truth from him. Just before the first lash strikes him,
however, Paul reveals his Roman citizenship, and the soldiers nervously
untie him lest they be punished for mistreating a citizen. It's a tough
day at work for the commanding officer.

As we recall from the tumult in Ephesus (19:23–41), the Romans
did not like rowdy public demonstrations, which tended to result
in uprisings, lost taxes, and other expensive inconveniences for the
management of an empire. The tribune, the leading military officer,
knows he cannot risk reigniting mob violence by releasing Paul. Nor
should he release anyone controversial from his custody, even a citizen,
without first determining whether the prisoner has done wrong or
poses an ongoing threat. In his primary responsibility to maintain
civic order, he's in a bit of a quandary.

In 22:30, the tribune decides to bring Paul before a council of Jerusalem's high-ranking Jewish religious leaders (sometimes referred
to by the Greek word for *council*: the Sanhedrin). This council has
little formal political or legal power; it is a loose collection of mostly
aristocratic advisers to the priest at the top of the pyramid, a high
priest named Ananias. (This is the third of three different men with
that name in Acts. It's our first encounter with this one.) High priests
at that time were more than religious functionaries. Ananias must
work in partnership with the tribune—and the tribune's boss, the
Roman governor of Judea—in a delicate governing alliance. The
Roman occupiers needed to show occasional sensitivity toward their
Judean subjects and keep them pacified without inciting grievances.
The temple-based priesthood had to help the Romans accomplish
this while trying to stay in the general population's good graces. The
alternative was to forfeit the influence and prerogatives Rome allowed
the high priestly families to enjoy.

Paul begins the session before the council willing to engage them;
he starts with a statement about his long-standing and ongoing faithfulness to the God of Israel. This hardly impresses Ananias, who

orders him struck on the mouth. Any hope for an unbiased assembly evaporates. That should surprise no one, since previous meetings of the high priest's council served as prefaces to the flogging of Peter and other apostles (5:27–41) and the murder of Stephen (6:12, 15); Paul faces a group of people Acts considers dangerous. He nevertheless strikes back verbally, and then his comment about not recognizing the high priest delivers a sarcastic barb: Ananias's actions render him unrecognizable to Paul; he hardly deserves the office he holds. So much for diplomacy.

Next, Paul gives his appraisal of the controversy: it centers on "the hope of the resurrection of the dead." He refers both to Jesus's resurrection and to the coming resurrection of all people, a hope grounded in the original Easter event (see 13:32–35; 17:31–32). Other speeches Paul gives during his custody reiterate his contention that Christian belief in Jesus's resurrection touches at the heart of Jewish traditions expecting God to raise the dead. Paul the Christian remains, he insists, a faithful Jew.

Maybe in this setting it's more fitting to consider him a faithful Pharisee. The council divides over the question of resurrection because teachings associated with the Pharisees (a growing lay movement within Judaism) affirmed the reality of life after death, while the Sadducees (a largely aristocratic group affiliated with the Jerusalem temple and chief priests) denied it. Paul's words frame the dissension according to what he thinks it is: an intra-Jewish dispute over how to understand God's intentions rightly. Paul's statement is less a crafty defense strategy and more an attempt to take a theological stand. If the Roman tribune thought a meeting with the council would lead to a unanimous decision on the question of "What has Paul done wrong, and why are some Jews upset with him?," he now knows better.

The scene descends into burlesque. The Pharisees and Sadducees on the council argue the warrants for believing in a postmortem resurrection. Imagine people yelling and throwing chairs at each other over a debate they engage in daily, all with full knowledge that their arguments will change no one's mind. Before they turn Paul into a human wishbone, the Roman soldiers hustle him back into their barracks for the night.

Then the Lord Jesus shows up.

Consider the wider circumstances. It appears Paul is becoming alienated from Judaism here in Jerusalem. More specifically, he's alienated from *some* circles of the local Jewish society. Although he preaches a message about God's determination to fulfill Jewish hopes, a segment of the general population rejects him. Now members of the official Jewish leadership spurn him and his message. He was physically shut out of the temple in 21:30 and now must reside with Roman soldiers—foreign occupiers—to keep alive. And why do none of the other disciples in Jerusalem materialize to lend support or encouragement? It all looks like failure, or perhaps a dead end.

Jesus shows up, then, at a critical moment.

His words endorse what Paul has just done: Paul has "testified," or given witness, for Jesus. He must eventually do the same in Rome, in line with what Paul resolved "in the Spirit" back in 19:21. Although isolated in custody, Paul is not alone, nor does he act purely of his own volition. Jesus's words to him imply a larger purpose at work, some kind of intention about his situation and a positive inevitability about what lies ahead—a transfer to Rome. Paul's custody represents a change from God's prior activity. God earlier delivered certain apostles, John, Peter, Paul, and Silas from previous imprisonments in jaw-dropping fashion. Jesus holds out no such hope to Paul here, yet he encourages him nevertheless. The same divine care that previously unlocked doors and frustrated authorities continues to abide with Paul. This care still accompanies Paul's efforts to bear witness to Jesus, even as he remains under guard in a condition that will last a long time before he makes it all the way to Rome in custody. Incarceration only appears to limit Paul. He still has work to do in this place.

In Roman hands, now and into the future, Paul circulates in uncertain conditions, made more striking through the narrative's flair for excitement. First, and made more threatening by an assassination conspiracy concocted by over forty people in 23:12–15, Paul continues to have dogged enemies outside the walls of his custody. This group of the Jerusalem-based Jewish authorities and their allies (just a group, not all of Jerusalem's people) will repeatedly apply pressure

until the Romans load their prisoner on a ship in Acts 27. Second,
Roman personnel serve simultaneously as his incarcerators and his
protectors. They aren't exactly sure what to do with him (23:23–30;
25:23–27), but they recognize him as political capital for their dealings
with the Jewish leaders in Jerusalem and they don't want to release
someone who might do damage to the empire's interests. For over
two years (24:27) they keep Paul in social quarantine in Caesarea, on
the Mediterranean coast, with occasional hearings that do little to
resolve the situation (24:1–23; 25:6–12). Third, Paul conducts himself
in exemplary fashion. When given opportunities to speak, to defend
himself, he addresses his faithfulness to the God of his ancestors. He
remains remarkably resolute.

We might say Paul remains heroic. He appears that way, given his
rhetorical panache and his cool demeanor through a variety of ups
and downs in Acts 23–26. But Jesus's visit, described so briefly in Acts
23:11, forces us to reevaluate any presumptions about Paul as a hero.

Jesus implies that Paul's detention and his actions as a prisoner fit
into a larger purpose. Because of this, Paul's cleverness, his clout as
a Roman citizen, his oratorical talents, the ambiguous legal-political
environment, and even his dumb luck fade from primary significance.
The larger story is that *God* authorizes Paul's work. His ability to
survive and bear witness points to divine care. Yes, Paul exemplifies
obedient and inspired witness amid hardship, but not necessarily as
an extraordinary individual or an irreplaceable captain.

Paul is therefore not a hero. He is still fulfilling the charge Jesus
gave in Acts 9:15–16: to bear Jesus's name. Only now he bears witness
to smaller and more influential audiences, still as God's instrument.
Also, now he can't go home at the end of each day.

The Christian church sometimes has difficulty with heroes. All
groups of people benefit from sound, inspirational leadership. Frequently through history, outstanding Christians with clear vision,
rugged commitment, and charisma have played pivotal roles in showing others, whether Christian or not, what the gospel of Jesus Christ
looks like when lived out. They guide the church away from error and
complacency. God becomes more clearly visible through their witness

and ministry. Yet we can find it difficult to let go of heroes, and we sometimes imagine the church's success depends on specific leaders. The story of Paul in custody asks us to think differently. It allows us to celebrate Paul's faithfulness and invites us to acclaim other saints who persevere in faithfulness despite setbacks. Yet it tells us, as it has before, that God will be discovered in various ways. No single form of ministry is required. No single leader is indispensable.

We need to consider this lesson carefully and intelligently. Some readers accuse Acts of a kind of bald, simplistic fatalism, as if it says, "Whatever happens, happens. That's how you discover God's will: it's what happens." This can become a cruel excuse for injustice and horrible suffering, if I have to believe God planned everything. It can also encourage irresponsible behavior or passivity, if people assume God just pulls the strings of our lives and we're merely hanging on for the ride.

As we have seen elsewhere, an alternate and more viable way of reading the book's accent on God's plan involves imagining what it means for God to accompany humanity in our toils and joys. What if God doesn't engineer our existence to accomplish specific, minutely defined ends? The Bible's talk about God's reliability and God's activity through our efforts pushes us to see God not as an invisible and irresistible force but on display in flesh-and-blood people and their attempts to express—to the degree anyone can—salvation's joy, justice, forgiveness, and renewal. This biblical language makes less a statement about how God operates and more a claim about how we come to glimpse God's presence and God's priorities in the midst of our activity and interpersonal interactions. Maybe a piece of the good news in Paul's case is that a person can glimpse this potential even while confined in custody.

A hero, then, isn't a person who can do things no one else can do. It's someone whose endurance, faith, and love shake the rest of us out of our lethargy just enough to imagine we're capable of doing similar things and thus always capable of experiencing God's presence in life-altering ways.

Acts 25:1–12

The Gospel and the Empire

> I am appealing to the emperor's tribunal; this is where I
> should be tried. (Acts 25:10)

If Jesus really wants Paul to bear witness in Rome, as Jesus himself
stated when he appeared in the Roman military barracks in Jerusalem
(23:11), why does it take Paul so long to get there? A brief overview
of Acts 23:12–24:27 will explain.

For a moment, it appeared Paul might get to Rome quickly. About
twenty-four hours after the vision in Jerusalem, Paul set out for Caesarea not as a free man but essentially as cargo in a high-security,
furtive military convoy arranged by the local Roman commanding
officer, who was determined to protect Paul from a plot against his
life. In Caesarea, however, the urgency suddenly vanished. Paul just
waited. The Romans held on to him, detained in the provincial government's main building. For two years. Acts describes very little of
what happens during that period.

At the beginning of Paul's stay in Caesarea, the provincial governor, Antonius Felix, a man history remembers as an incompetent and
sometimes severe administrator, held a hearing involving Paul and
his accusers. These accusers, the high priest along with some officials
and a top-flight legal counsel, traveled from Jerusalem, over fifty miles
away. Felix made no decision about Paul's case, although afterward he

had frequent discussions with Paul. He also hoped Paul or his allies might offer a bribe for his release. Paul expressed no desire to leave, and Felix understood him to be a valuable prisoner for conciliating the chief priests in Jerusalem. Two years passed. Then, immediately following Felix's removal by order of Emperor Nero, Porcius Festus arrived on the scene as the new governor.

As soon as Festus assumes office at the beginning of this passage, the chief priests complain to him about Paul, and he convenes a hearing in Caesarea. The scene is brief. Paul flatly denies having broken Jewish law or having offended the Roman emperor. Festus would be most concerned about the latter. Paul's denial is technically correct: in Acts he has not set out to injure the emperor's reputation or prerogatives. He must know, nevertheless, that his ministry (especially as described in Acts 16–19) regularly caused controversy about the gospel's perceived implications for Roman society and the empire's values. A consequence of the gospel, at least in the perspective of many in Acts who hear Paul's proclamation, is that it challenges and potentially destabilizes aspects of the Roman cultural status quo—maybe not in a revolutionary vein, but in the ways the gospel disrupts its adherents' lives, allegiances, and priorities. Everywhere.

The question of whether Paul's missionary activity has political or anti-imperial ramifications beckons us to consider the men who determine Paul's fate in Acts 24–26. Felix and Festus were the highest-ranking Roman officials in Judea. They were governors (technically, procurators) of this Roman province, with virtually the same responsibilities and broad powers Pontius Pilate held a few decades earlier. They directly represented the emperor himself, defending his interests and safeguarding the empire's values. Their office gave them tremendous authority, allowing them almost total discretion over judicial hearings, judgments, and sentencing. Paul stands in front of the most powerful people in his world, with few rights and little leverage.

At the same time, governors had territories to manage and tense political alliances to maintain. Therefore, while Festus seems rather uninterested in what might warrant Paul's release or conviction, he keenly recognizes Paul's value for keeping the temple-based aristocracy in his debt. This nuisance named Paul might make a fine diplomatic gift to the new governor's subjugated people in that sometimes volatile city named Jerusalem. So Festus raises the possibility of transferring Paul back there for a substantial trial.

Paul recognizes Festus's proposal as a trap, a virtual guarantee of an unfair process. He may also perceive—as the narrator indicates and whether the governor knows it or not—that he would be killed before even reaching Jerusalem. Unwilling to be a pawn sacrificed in a game of political favors among society's elite powerbrokers, he demands to make his case elsewhere: Paul insists on having the emperor himself issue Rome's judgment about Paul and his activities. He will make his full defense in the ears of the man at the center of the Roman Empire.

While it is not clear that Paul or any other defendant in his situation would really have had the inalienable right to make such an appeal, Festus sees it as something he must do in this case (reaffirmed in 25:21; 26:31–32). Festus wants first one more hearing to help him figure out what to tell the emperor about Paul (25:25–27). After that, however, Festus's decree will go forward: Paul's next destination will be Rome.

How, then, does Paul finally make it to Rome? The literal answer is: by ship. But the question's real interest lies in understanding the forces that bring him there. Jesus's words to Paul in 23:11 suggest God plans to get Paul to Rome. Festus's decree, in response to Paul's appeal, suggests Roman authority determines Paul will go.

Of course, both can be true: God and Roman authorities can both play parts, and we need not imagine we can finely parse the relationship or the difference between divine will and human authority, as Acts understands these things. People have been trying that for centuries without much luck, and Acts seems happy to assert the reality of both without worrying about any supposed conflict (see 2:22–23, concerning Jesus's death as the result of God's intentions *and* human agency). Instead, the point worth examining now is the specific matter of how Acts presents Paul's transfer to Rome: it is part of God's plan for him, and the Roman political system makes it happen.

Everything about Acts 21–28, the story of Paul's prolonged custody, holds the power of the Roman Empire in front of readers. Acts
provides constant reminders that Paul now operates in the rarefied
air of elite, powerful culture.

- A commanding officer intends to torture Paul in Jerusalem
  (22:23–29)
- A massive military escort oversees Paul's transfer to Caesarea
  (23:23)
- Two provincial governors, Felix and Festus, pay attention to
  Paul's case (chaps. 23–25)
- High-stakes political maneuvers almost deliver Paul into an
  ambush (23:12–22; 25:1–12)
- At a hearing introduced with majestic pomp, Paul delivers a
  speech to Festus, a Roman-appointed ruler (a client king) over
  parts of Palestine named Herod Agrippa II, Agrippa's wife Bernice, and a collection of other Roman bigwigs (25:23)

Rome's representatives deal with Paul now. He resides in their
custody, and they will determine with whom he can share his message. Rome will judge whether Paul should live or die.

Through it all, nevertheless, Paul continues to speak about Jesus
Christ and describe his own missionary activity as lived faithfulness
to the God of Israel. Even if he can no longer speak his message in
public, he can do so in his restricted environment, bringing the gospel
into social settings not previously accessible to him. In doing so, Paul
frustrates the authorities' intentions of keeping him quarantined. Paul
adapts to these new conditions. His mission continues. The word of
God finds new avenues to travel.

This observation goes beyond saying Acts counsels us to smile our
way through an ugly situation. Paul's ability to persevere as a missionary and his eventual transfer to Rome say something about who God
is and how God should be regarded in relation to the Roman Empire.

Paul exercises substantial control over how he, the prisoner, is
treated. His words and insight determine a large measure of what will
happen to him. His knowledge of an imminent attack prompted the

Roman military to hustle him from Jerusalem to Caesarea (23:16–24). His quick-thinking appeal means his case can go to Rome, so he can testify before the emperor himself. These evasive reactions effectively frustrate the intentions of some of the most powerful people in Judea, the Roman governor and the temple leadership. All of this comes in the wake of the previously announced divine intention of Paul going to Rome (23:11), but it comes as structures of Roman authority make that intention a reality. While the Romans act to control Paul, God's will nevertheless comes to fruition.

Is God then controlling people's minds and actions? Not necessarily. Instead, Acts has us see the Roman political system, in all its vast powers, as not nearly as absolute and dominant as it may appear on the surface. Acts does this by portraying Paul as very influential over his legal proceedings, even though a prisoner like him would at that time in Judea have had very little control over those processes. With dramatic flair, Acts insists once again that announcing and living out the word of God can prove disruptive to all involved. Paul, empowered by God, cannot truly be overpowered even by the priorities and muscle of those people and structures that purport to control human societies. Jesus is Lord, not Caesar. God's will prevails, whether the emperor's will concurs or not.

This idea of the gospel finding positive opportunities despite the counteracting forces of political suppression can be pushed too far. For example, it should not imply that James's death in 12:2 accomplishes the will of God, that God *uses* a Roman official to snuff out an apostle for some good reason. Nor should it promise never-ending success and triumph for those who minister in Jesus's name. Paul will eventually die, after all. Acts implies and later Christian tradition claims he died in Rome under the authority of Emperor Nero. Acts does not hand out "get out of jail free" cards to Christians. It does not deny the reality of suffering and defeat.

Instead, the point to notice here is that Acts depicts Paul's transfer to Rome in revealing ways. The subtleties of the narrative ask us to look at Paul's tense and vulnerable situation and see more than Roman power having its way with him. We should see more than

Paul surviving through his gifts and cleverness. Acts again issues a statement, a verdict of its own, about where true power lies.

Even the Roman Empire, one of the most dominant and apparently irresistible political forces the world has ever known, appears ripe for Paul to exploit to fulfill God's intentions. Even if Acts conveys this point by implication rather than overt demonstration, the point still serves the wider story about an intrusive God and a disruptive gospel. Once again, this gospel affects the environment in which it finds itself. Indeed, it can outrun and potentially surmount any system of government—or any structure, any institution, any convention, any person—that presumes to make the rules about what's possible and about whose intentions must ultimately be realized.

Acts 27–28

Open Horizons

And so we came to Rome. (Acts 28:14)

Sometimes an ending ties a story's many strands of plotlines and characters into a neat resolution. Sometimes it only tugs on those strands, leaving them extended to turn readers outward to imagine new directions and expanding possibilities for a still unfolding, not-yet-finished story. No surprise: Acts has the second kind of ending.

Acts moves toward its conclusion with several accounts of high adventure. If it were a feature film, we might suspect the producers had been under budget and worried it needed more excitement, and so they squeezed in a few more action scenes. When Paul and a larger party of prisoners, soldiers, and commercial sailors depart Caesarea for Rome, Acts takes its time describing the early, meandering legs of the sea voyage, making most of us realize how little we know about the geography of the eastern Mediterranean Sea (27:1–8). After that, however, the tale turns exciting: disagreements with the ship's captain, a violent storm, an incapacitated ship, failing food supplies, jettisoned cargo, a dramatic swim to shore, marooned travelers, friendly island natives, a venomous snakebite, miraculous preservation of life, travel on a different ship, and a splendid reception from Roman believers. The account ratchets up the drama and makes readers wait a little longer to see whether Paul will make it to Rome and, if so, what will happen once he gets there.

Through all the suspense, it can be difficult to remember that Paul is still a prisoner. After all, his legal situation never reached resolution in Caesarea. Acts 26 ended with a grandiose hearing in which Paul summarized a number of themes that had been key in his ministry—his missionary work as his faithfulness to God, his understanding of the gospel as fulfilling the Jewish scriptures, and the resurrection of Jesus as an act of God to bring light to all peoples. But the scene only prolonged Paul's case. In fact, Agrippa thought Paul could have been set free, had he not appealed to the emperor (26:32). So Paul's jeopardy remains, as does his custody.

Despite the legal predicament, Paul's voyage and eventual reception in Rome are narrated with accents on his autonomy, not his limitations. Several times during the ill-fated trip Paul becomes the source of his fellow travelers' security when danger arises. Not a good-luck charm, Paul serves as a tangible expression of God's active care for people—even the military escorts—and the adventure reiterates God's determination to have Paul bear witness to Jesus in the imperial capital.

The narrative does not let us lose sight of the soldiers, led by a centurion named Julius, and their responsibility over Paul and other prisoners (27:6, 11, 31–32, 42–44). At the same time, Paul repeatedly assumes prominence over his keepers and the professional sailors. He advises them, unsuccessfully, on safe travel. He rebukes and encourages them even as he, correctly, anticipates shipwreck. He commands them, accurately, about how to remain alive. He distributes food to all 276 people on board, making us wonder how a captive gets to exercise such important authority over supplies and why the ship's owner and pilot fade from our view. No wonder Julius protects Paul's life when the other soldiers decide it would be a good idea to kill all the prisoners instead of risking their escape when everyone must abandon ship.

The sea voyage resembles Paul's hearing before the high priest and his council back in 22:30–23:11. Back then, it appeared Paul might be torn to pieces by the disputing council; now on the water, forces of nature threaten his life. The storm carries symbolic value. Will it judge Paul guilty and annihilate him? Has he done something wrong, à la the prophet Jonah, whose disobedience led to a tempest at sea? Paul cannot control the wind and waves, and so his survival suggests God protects him and declares his innocence. The storm may force everyone into the chaotic waters, but it cannot disrupt God's objective. As Jesus endorsed Paul's witness in 23:11, likewise Paul's report of an angelic visitor on the ship restates God's intention to have him get to Rome, as well as God's intention to preserve each soul on the ship.

First, they need to get off of Malta, a small island south of Sicily. The trial-by-nature theme continues there when Paul, helpfully gathering wood for a fire, gets bitten by a snake in exchange for his efforts. The Maltese natives recognize the snake as poisonous and conclude this prisoner is receiving his comeuppance. When nothing happens to Paul, they change their opinion and assume him to be a god. Paul doesn't correct them, as in 14:8–20. Presumably, by this point in the tortuous journey, he'd rather let it go, find a warm bed, and get some rest.

The forced layover in Malta goes well. Paul meets the island's leader, heals his father's illness, and cures other islanders suffering from diseases. In exchange, the Maltese give the whole shipwrecked group all they need to survive for three months, plus provisions for a trip to Italy on another ship that is wintering at the island. It's good to have Paul along for the ride when traveling in potentially dangerous settings.

Uncharacteristically, Acts mentions no preaching on Malta. Paul's role here is to be a means by which people—he and his co-travelers—are preserved and equipped to complete the journey. Paul's task as a witness involves more than words and persuasion. The church's business is not merely to enlarge itself or to serve others for the purposes of drawing a crowd to hear the gospel. Paul performs acts of mercy for the islanders' own sake, offering concrete expressions of God's care and salvation.

The sea voyage continues beyond Malta, punctuated with stops in different ports to maintain the suspense. When Paul and his guardians disembark in Puteoli, on the western coast of the Italian Peninsula, we learn the gospel message arrived in Rome sometime before he does;

Christians are already there. He, presumably with the soldiers, stays with believers in Puteoli for a week. Next, Christians from Rome travel south to meet him in the Forum of Appius and in Three Taverns (forty-three-mile and thirty-three-mile journeys, respectively). The language describing these gatherings suggests more than a simple hello. It can indicate a festive welcome of a celebrated dignitary. This detail provides one more sign of Paul's importance, but that importance serves a purpose beyond aggrandizing Paul. Given what we've seen in the ways Acts 21–28 presents Paul, his reception redounds to God's credit. God's intention to have Paul go to Rome finally comes to completion. Paul's arrival means God's faithfulness proves itself yet again, giving Paul the courage to face whatever comes next.

Once in Rome, Paul settles into his own lodgings. House arrest under a soldier's watch in a private residence requires Paul to provide for himself. Acts describes two separate conversations he hosts in his home with leaders of the local Jewish population.

With complaints against him having persisted unabated for a two-year period in Caesarea, perhaps what Paul hears in the first conversation surprises him: the local Jews have not received reports about him. This affords him a bit of a fresh start with this audience, even though they admit "this sect" Paul represents suffers from a bad reputation.

The second meeting lasts a full day and involves "great numbers" of visitors. Paul tells them about Jesus, anchoring his presentation in the language and witness of Jewish scriptures (the Law and the Prophets), although Acts does not reveal the specific texts under discussion. He convinces some of his audience, but this important detail becomes overshadowed by his sharp response to those who don't believe his message. As they leave his dwelling, he hurls at them words taken from Isaiah 6:9–10 (specifically, from the Greek translation of that part of the Hebrew scriptures). They are harsh words, accusing an audience of obstinacy and an inability to hear the truth. Then Paul tells them God's salvation has been sent to gentiles, and "they will listen."

This statement marks the third time in Acts that Paul, in response to a Jewish audience's refusal to heed him to his satisfaction, tells them he will preach the gospel to gentiles. After each of the previous two instances (13:46–47; 18:5–6), Paul cooled off and soon resumed preaching to Jewish groups, as well as to gentiles. Notice in 28:28 that he does not say God rescinds the promise of salvation from Jews, only that gentiles will receive salvation too. Paul stops far short of claiming God has cut ties with Jews. It's denunciation, not damnation. His problem is with this particular group of people, here in his rented home, who seem unable to accept what he has to say. He can't get them to see the gospel's connection to Israel's hopes regarding God's promised salvation. They also don't see what he sees, that his struggles and current incarceration demonstrate his firm commitment to those same hopes.

As is often the case, Paul gets the final word. By citing Isaiah and declaring that he speaks in agreement with the Holy Spirit, Paul utters a word of judgment. In a twist, the defendant renders a verdict. Again, Paul is no overwhelmed or victimized prisoner.

Acts rapidly brings the book to an end with a two-verse conclusion. Paul remains in his rented dwelling for two years, but he nevertheless enjoys continued access to the outside world. He receives people, "all who came to him," presumably Jews and gentiles alike. The final two words in Acts (a single word in the book's original Greek) characterize this period of Paul's custody: "without hindrance." He bears witness to Jesus and the kingdom of God freely. "Without hindrance" means the Roman authorities do not restrict who may visit him; it also means God's presence with Paul continues without restraint. Although caged, Paul is not confined. Better, the gospel he preaches remains unconfined, even beyond the boundaries of the story now coming to its conclusion.

A statement of boldness and freedom, and not the certain, pending death of Paul, hangs in the air as the book ends. Yes, Paul remains under guard, and so Acts does not entirely shield us from Paul's persistent legal jeopardy. Still, in opting not to narrate Paul's death, the conclusion keeps the focus on the word of God, the preached message, not the preacher.

The story's main character was never Paul to begin with.

Nor Peter.

Nor Philip.

Nor Priscilla.

All these people matter, but only insofar as they serve, speak, and embody the word of God. Through their witness, and even sometimes without their direct involvement, the word of God perseveres. It will persevere when they are dead and gone. Acts concludes with a brief report about Paul's ongoing preaching about the kingdom of God, precisely because these circumstances reiterate one of the central points Acts seeks to make about God: God won't permit bearing witness to the kingdom's new realities ever to come to an end.

By the time Paul begins his sea voyage in Acts 27, readers should be used to the book's pattern of manufactured and amazing happy endings. Ancient dramas were sometimes fond of employing a convention called "*deus ex machina*" (Latin for "a god out of a machine"), in which a deity, character, or detail bursts into a story at the last minute to produce a solution to what looked like a hopeless situation. It allows a story to build suspense, but it can leave audiences and readers incredulous, especially when the move is contrived or simplistic. Acts takes this risk, over and over again. Paul just won't die. God has other plans.

Why does Acts attribute such good fortune to Paul the prisoner? Not because he is especially clever. Why does Acts speak of God protecting him? Not because God needs him. Ever since Acts 21, when Paul returned to Jerusalem, Acts has given readers glimpses behind the curtain, referring to God residing in the machine, to show us forces arrayed against Paul as well as to characterize Paul's eventual arrival in Rome as an act of God and another step forward for the message of salvation. The story might have provided merely a legal and procedural account of Paul's final judicial challenges and travels, but then we might miss the sense of a larger purpose in what happens to Paul. His relocation to Rome means something, according to Acts. The sheer presence of Paul in Rome, still spreading and embodying the word of God, endorses the things he says and does. These endorsements underscore God's intentions, expressed in the gospel Paul preaches.

In the final chapters of Acts, a note of sadness accompanies the confidence. Paul remains in custody, and his death appears imminent. At the same time, Christian witnesses reside in the heart of the empire. Paul's relative freedoms minimize any sense of his subjection to the empire's absolute supremacy, represented by soldiers who only ostensibly control his circumstances. Paul repeatedly insists that he does not reject Judaism but rather sees the gospel of Jesus Christ as God's fulfillment of long-standing Jewish hopes.

Those points of confidence reverberate with the book's many assertions that God is able to disrupt the obstacles poised to hinder our opportunities to encounter God and live into the salvation God provides. The book does not guarantee rescue, but it does reassure us that encountering God is never beyond possibility. Sadness, struggle, and even shipwrecks always continue, but they won't be the final act. At least, not when we consider the grand scheme of things. God will yet intrude. The story of God's salvation always extends further than the book of Acts can map it.

How could anyone not want to see this kind of story continue?

Conclusion

They . . . examined the scriptures every day to see whether
these things were so. (Acts 17:11)

When accusations against them in the city of Thessalonica force Paul
and Silas to travel fifty miles to Beroea, a city off the beaten track of
the major trade routes in Macedonia, members of the local synagogue
and others generally welcome their message. The positive reception
remains short lived, for antagonists follow them there and stir up
the crowds so that Paul must be spirited out of town for his safety.

In this account, told in 17:10–15, those in Beroea who respond
positively to the gospel before the uproar brings the scene to a sudden
close include men and women, Jews and gentiles, people of various
social classes. Although we learn none of their names and no details of their personal stories, Acts gives a brief description of their
enthusiasm: "These Jews were more receptive than those in Thessalonica, for they welcomed the message very eagerly and examined
the scriptures every day to see whether these things were so. Many
of them therefore believed, including not a few Greek women and
men of high standing" (17:11–12).

Commitment to the good news in Jesus Christ does not come in-
stantaneously to these "receptive" people. Nor do supernatural signs
and wonders cause them to express faith. For them, it's a process. It's
about being attentive. Their initial response to the gospel message
leads them to examine the scriptures with energy, repeatedly, and

together to confirm for themselves whether what they are hearing is so. "Therefore," Acts says, because of their reading, many people come to believe.

If our exploration of Acts has been successful, it will likewise encourage you to examine the Scriptures—the book of Acts and the other biblical writings. Acts describes people bearing witness to Jesus, and, as we have seen, Acts also bears witness itself to Jesus's continuing presence and influence. Presumably the author of Acts wanted readers, back around the year 100, to find comfort and confidence in understanding God as a *present* reality in their lives, not just to look into the past to see God as a source of power for Jesus's original followers.

Reading Scripture can have similar results for us: we read to learn how people of faith thought about God in ancient times, but in reading we also find ourselves considering where and how God might be encountered in our own experiences. Examining the Scriptures can go hand in hand with examining our own lives. As a result, we might discover God in ways both familiar and new, both comforting and disruptive, both straightforward and mysterious.

We read Scripture today much differently than people did when Acts was written. We ask different questions when we read. Sometimes we see different things. We understand the world differently, at least in some respects. We may hold different basic assumptions about God and about the nature of virtue. We find some details of the book's depiction of God delightful, others objectionable. We also read the Scriptures, including the Acts of the Apostles, in light of almost two thousand years of accumulated insight. This insight, which we sometimes refer to as "tradition," helps us read; tradition puts us into conversation with those who have gone before us and been attentive to God's activity in their midst. Tradition reminds us we do not read in isolation, and it encourages us to examine the Scriptures in ways like the people of Beroea probably do in Acts 17: with others in groups.

The long arc of tradition also reminds us to read the Scriptures with a degree of openness—openness to learning from others and attentiveness to all sorts of questions, including these: What if God is indeed like that? Or not like that? What would it mean for me? What would it mean for my neighbors, both those nearby and those far away?

Our responses to those questions may disrupt our lives and beliefs, in both small and large ways. Our responses may alter how we think about the world and our place in it. They may change us, lifting us up or taking us down a few pegs.

If any of these things happen, the book of Acts will encourage us to conclude that an intrusive God was somehow involved, trying to get our attention.

For Further Reading

In the preface I noted that many people played a part in this book. Some of them are authors whose contributions have deeply influenced how I think about Acts and the Bible as a whole. My book's format doesn't allow me to note every place where other scholars' insights have proven helpful, so I name some of their writings here to acknowledge my debt to them and to offer suggestions to anyone interested in continuing to explore Acts along lines similar to those I've drawn throughout this book. Not everything on my list expects its readers to possess familiarity with biblical scholarship, its jargon, and its methods.

There are plenty of worthy commentaries on Acts in print. Here I recommend only a select few.

Chance, J. Bradley. *Acts.* Smyth & Helwys Bible Commentary. Macon, GA: Smyth & Helwys, 2007. This commentary assumes little background knowledge in academic biblical studies. It devotes much attention to how Acts speaks about discipleship, testimony, and the relationship between divine will and human freedom.

Gaventa, Beverly Roberts. *Acts.* Abingdon New Testament Commentary. Nashville: Abingdon, 2003. Teachers and preachers in particular can learn much from Gaventa's careful attention to the narrative character and theological message of Acts.

González, Justo L. *Acts: The Gospel of the Spirit.* Maryknoll, NY: Orbis, 2001. González writes particularly for Protestants living in Latin America and the United States. He reads Acts with an eye toward the book's relevance for those audiences in the contemporary world.

Pervo, Richard I. *Acts.* Hermeneia. Minneapolis: Fortress, 2009. If there's a question about a historical dimension of Acts—concerning the story it tells, the history behind the book, and how other ancient literature and ideas might have influenced it—chances are good that this very thorough, sophisticated, and technical commentary offers an answer to it.

Spencer, F. Scott. *Journeying through Acts: A Literary-Cultural Reading.* Peabody, MA: Hendrickson, 2004. Spencer traverses Acts with great creativity and insight into the book's narrative dynamics. He attends closely to the social world that Acts depicts.

Tannehill, Robert C. *The Narrative Unity of Luke-Acts: A Literary Interpretation.* Vol. 2, *The Acts of the Apostles.* Minneapolis: Fortress, 1990. This study of Acts is especially helpful in its analysis of the conflicts that arise from the proclamation of the gospel and the crises that emerge as the early church expands.

Other studies have taught me much about how best to approach certain topics or passages.

Berrigan, Daniel. *Whereon to Stand: The Acts of the Apostles and Ourselves.* Eugene, OR: Wipf & Stock, 1991. Can Acts be interpreted in a poetic vein? Absolutely, if Berrigan is the interpreter. This Jesuit priest and longtime public advocate for peace, disarmament, and justice reflects on Acts in connection to the contemporary struggles that have marked his life and ministry.

Finger, Reta Halteman. *Of Widows and Meals: Communal Meals in the Book of Acts.* Grand Rapids: Eerdmans, 2007. This book addresses questions related to descriptions of community life in the early chapters of Acts and especially the crisis that develops in 6:1–7. It considers historical, literary, and logistic evidence for understanding how the earliest church fed and served its members and for determining whether widows in the church really were as powerless as is often assumed.

Garrett, Susan R. *The Demise of the Devil: Magic and the Demonic in Luke's Writings.* Minneapolis: Fortress, 1989. The subtitle announces the topic. Garrett guides us toward a better understanding of some of the obstacles the gospel encounters in Acts.

Johnson, Luke Timothy. *Scripture and Discernment: Decision-Making in the Church.* Nashville: Abingdon, 1996. In this engaging book written for popular audiences, Johnson explores passages from Acts in which key decisions are made, such as 6:1–7; 10:1–11:18; and 15:1–35. He interprets them carefully and discusses how Christians can conduct communal discernment in ways that honor and clarify their own theological commitments.

Marguerat, Daniel. *The First Christian Historian: Writing the "Acts of the Apostles."* Society for New Testament Studies Monograph Series 121. Cambridge: Cambridge University Press, 2002. The scholarly essays in this collection have profoundly shaped how I understand the genre of Acts and the way the book describes events in its efforts to convey a theological vision.

Reimer, Ivoni Richter. *Women in the Acts of the Apostles: A Feminist Liberation Perspective.* Minneapolis: Fortress, 1995. Several passages featuring women characters receive in-depth treatment in this book, which explores the relevant historical landscape and rigorously analyzes the women's portrayals from a feminist outlook.

Seim, Turid Karlsen. *The Double Message: Patterns of Gender in Luke and Acts.* Nashville: Abingdon, 1994. This scholarly exploration of the depictions of women and their roles in Luke and Acts argues that competing impulses can be found in both books; sometimes they reinforce traditional gender roles, and sometimes they suggest the possibility of liberation from the constraints of those roles.

Skinner, Matthew L. *The Trial Narratives: Conflict, Power, and Identity in the New Testament.* Louisville: Westminster John Knox, 2010. This earlier and more technical book explains the foundations of my thinking about all the scenes in Acts in which someone is put on trial or faces legal jeopardy.

Spencer, F. Scott. *Dancing Girls, Loose Ladies, and Women of the Cloth: The Women in Jesus's Life*. New York: Continuum, 2004. A few chapters in this smart book treat scenes from Acts, including the raising of Tabitha/Dorcas (Acts 9) and the slave girl with the Python spirit (Acts 16).

Finally, if you want to read shorter articles or essays, and if you have access to the journals or collections in which they appear, here are some that continue to capture my imagination. Now that I've written this book, I see how truly influential these continue to be for me.

Alexander, Loveday. "Fact, Fiction and the Genre of Acts." *New Testament Studies* 44 (1998): 380–99. Modern people sometimes get caught up in thinking that an episode in a book like Acts must be *either* fictional *or* factual. Alexander considers Acts in light of ancient historians' conceptions of history and explains how this either-or way of thinking cannot adequately explain what Acts is up to.

Alexander, Loveday. "'This Is That': The Authority of Scripture in the Acts of the Apostles." *Princeton Seminary Bulletin* 25 (2004): 189–204. I'll read anything Loveday Alexander writes about Acts, because she's such a careful, knowledgeable reader of texts and the ancient world. This article guides my thoughts about what we can learn from the citation of Joel 2:28–32a in Peter's Pentecost sermon in Acts 2.

Gaventa, Beverly Roberts. "Toward a Theology of Acts: Reading and Rereading." *Interpretation* 42 (1988): 146–57. This groundbreaking article insists that our attempts to describe the theology on display in Acts must attend carefully to the narrative dynamics that make this story what it is.

Minear, Paul S. "Dear Theo: The Kerygmatic Intention and Claim of the Book of Acts." *Interpretation* 27 (1973): 131–50. Minear describes Acts as an example of participating in "the continuing conversation between the word of God and the people of God," a book meant to tell its earliest ancient audiences about how they connect to Jesus and to the life and witness of the Christian communities he brought into being.

Skinner, Matthew L. "Acts." In *Theological Bible Commentary*, edited by Gail R. O'Day and David L. Petersen, 359–71. Louisville: Westminster John Knox, 2009. If you'd like a slightly more academic account of what I think are the theological contributions of the book of Acts, this piece offers that. No surprise: I contend that the book's central theological impulse is the depiction of the word of God persisting throughout the various social and cultural circumstances in which Jesus's followers found themselves.

Walton, Steve. "The State They Were In: Luke's View of the Roman Empire." In *Rome in the Bible and the Early Church*, edited by Peter Oakes, 1–41. Grand Rapids: Baker Academic, 2002. Scholars vigorously debate how the book of Acts regards the Roman Empire and what perspectives it takes on how Christians should navigate life as imperial subjects and citizens. Walton's essay offers a clear and well-reasoned overview of most of the options proposed prior to 2002.

Subject Index

Scripture Index

Romans

Galatians